One Man's Journey

by

Vernon Carter, Ed.D.

Memoir
BOOKS
Chico, CA

Contents

Foreword

Every person in our world is unique. Each one has a life story, a story to tell. Each life is a journey. Everyone could write a story about his trip through life. Some might be short stories and of interest only to his children or immediate family; some might have a broader interest. Many stories have been written about the lives of famous people. Some writers have written their stories so well that they have become famous as a result.

My story is being laid down primarily for my family. It may be of some interest to friends and others, but that is not its purpose. Travel has played a big part in my life, so the metaphor of life's journey has a double meaning. The essays in this book were written individually, so some things I say are repeated throughout for those who pick chapters to read randomly.

The gist of the story is simple. The early divorce of my parents seemed to put me at a disadvantage from the beginning. I'm sure I had a feeling about this handicap from an early age, since I was deprived of a father figure in my life. The journey then was to overcome this challenge and to move onward and upward by my own efforts. In a nutshell, this is a rags to riches story; a rising from the depths of the Depression (1928). It is a story of achieving goals, one step at a time, and moving ahead slowly but surely.

The goals were always set in attainable increments, which is important for success.

My journey got off to a slow start due to the divorce of my parents when I was five years old. The only good part about it was that it resulted in a train trip. This was my first journey, from Kansas City, Missouri, to Los Angeles, California.

Chapter 4

My Birth

I was born. That much was certain, but the details are rather sketchy. I have never had any real information about my birth. I don't know whether I was born in a hospital or at home. None of this information was passed down through our family. I think the reason for this was that my mother never said much about her life during those five years leading up to the divorce. My dad must have had an affair with his secretary and then they married after the divorce. They had a pleasant life for thirty years or so until she died.

I will give my mother a lot of credit. She never said a bad word about our father to my sister or me. She never bad-mouthed him. In fact, she never said much about the whole divorce situation.

Upon researching my birth certificate many years later, I discovered that I was born at 3:05 P.M. and delivered by a physician. I still don't know whether it was at home or in a hospital, but assume that it was probably in a hospital.

Calvin Coolidge was president when I was born. Harding died in office in 1923. Coolidge was sworn in on August 1, just before I was born in September.

Chapter 5

My Earliest Memory

My earliest childhood memory was a trauma that occurred when I was three or four years old. We lived in a fairly nice middle class neighborhood in a single-family home in Kansas City, Missouri. The homes there in the1920s did not have fences around the yards as they do in much of California today. There were nice grassy areas between all of the homes, which made for a wonderful park or play area for the children.

I enjoyed playing out there with the neighborhood kids. One day, I got into an argument with another young boy. Maybe he was the neighborhood bully, I don't know, but I was always good as gold! He picked up a garden hand sickle, which looked like the one on the Communist logo, and chased me home. I just made it inside the back screen door. I turned around to look at him from the safety, I thought, of my back porch. I might have stuck my tongue out at him, I don't remember. He was determined in his pursuit. He swung the sickle at me and it went through the screen door into my upper right arm an inch or so.

There was blood all over the place and I have a half-inch scar on my bicep that I have carried with me ever since. I don't know what happened to the other kid. I hope he is still in jail!

Chapter 6

Mabel Jadwin and Edwin Wilbur Carter

Mabel Jadwin, daughter of a Kansas City police captain, and Edwin Wilbur Carter were married around 1920 in Kansas City, Missouri. They both worked for a milk processing company called a creamery in those days. I was their first child, born in September 1923 and my sister Shirley was born in November 1925. My parents—the Carters—had a good life. They lived in a single-family home in a middle-class neighborhood. They played bridge often with friends in the evening and Mabel took care of the household and their children while Ed continued working. The Carters were divorced in 1928 when I was five years old. Ed found a secretary, Alice, who apparently was more to his liking, and married her. Mabel and the two children moved to California to live with Mabel's sister Aunt Julie, and Julia's husband Uncle Jack.

That was the end of a happy life for Mabel. She never had another serious male friend all of her life, and devoted her time to raising the children as best she could. I give her a lot of credit for never saying anything negative about my father. During the Depression, I had no knowledge of Ed ever paying any alimony or child support, but Mabel still didn't badmouth him in any way. The family kept in touch with Ed by mail on birthdays and other events such as Christmas.

Ed moved to Moberly, Missouri, with Alice where he became half owner of a coal mine.

Mabel, Shirley, and I moved back to Kansas City in 1937 for a short period. We lived there just one year before moving back to California. I graduated from Central Junior High School in Kansas City in February 1938, and Ed came up from Moberly for that occasion. It was nice to have both parents there for that event.

When I was ready to go to Occidental College in 1941, the tuition was $400 a year which was a lot of money in those days. I had been driving a laundry truck all summer at the rate of 35 cents an hour, and had been saving my money for college. I had earned about $200 and was $200 short, so I wrote to my dad asking him for the $200. That was the only time in my life I asked my dad for any money. Ed sent me the $200 right away, which was much appreciated. Ed received a thank you letter from me very promptly.

When I moved into the fraternity house as a freshman at Oxy, Mabel and Shirley found an apartment together close by, and Mabel held a job off and on for most of the rest of her life. At one point she worked for a trucking company and had to join the Teamsters' Union and go to Union meetings at least quarterly. Shirley and I teased Mabel about being a teamster.

When I married Bev Gillett we bought our first home in Reseda, California, in 1949 while I was a teacher and football coach at Marshall High School in Hollywood. The house cost $9,900 and we were mighty proud of our new home. It had two bedrooms and one bath.

In 1952 I applied for and was awarded a Fulbright grant to be an exchange teacher in the Netherlands for a year. We had two children, Bob and Deanna, at that time. The children were two and three years old. We drove across country and sold our car in New Jersey before sailing for Holland. We arranged to stop by Moberly on the way across country to see Ed and Alice. This was the first time we had met Alice, and I hadn't seen Ed since my junior high graduation in 1938, a thirteen-year gap in time. We had a nice visit with the senior Carters who were most gracious to all of us. This was an opportunity for Ed to meet his first two grandchildren. When we returned from Holland in the late summer of 1953, we stopped in Moberly again for a brief visit with Ed and Alice on the way home.

Some time later after Shirley had married Bill Grindrod and Mabel was living alone in an apartment, Mabel's health began to fail. At that time Bev and I brought her to Reseda to live with us. We enclosed the back porch and this became her room.

Bev gave her mother-in-law the utmost love, kindness, and care in her decline. Bev had known Mabel before she knew me. Bev and Shirley were sorority sisters and Bev had spent a lot of time at Mabel's house, across the street from Occidental. Mabel passed away in our home in Reseda. I always appreciated the kindness and care that Bev gave to my mother in the final days of her life.

Aunt Julia had worked as a secretary for Jack Roth in a stockbroker business. Roth had a few problems and was sent to San Quentin for a few years. Julia stood by him all the way and testified in court on his behalf. As a result, they remained good friends for the rest of their lives. When Mr. Roth got out of prison he got a job as manager of the renowned Hollywood Cemetery where many famous Hollywood people and actors are buried. Rudolph Valentino is buried there and also Marilyn Monroe. Joe DiMaggio sent flowers to Monroe's grave for many years.

I don't know the details, but I believe that Jack Roth gave Aunt Julia three crypts in the mausoleum there. At any rate, Uncle Jack, Aunt Julia, and Mabel are all side by side in that mausoleum.

Alice, Ed's second wife, passed away and Ed was retired and living alone in Moberly. Ed had severe emphysema, had difficulty breathing, and his health was failing. Bev and I invited Ed to come out to California to live with us in Reseda. We soon found that we didn't have enough room to accommodate this new family member, so we purchased a new larger home in Canoga Park, a little further out in the San Fernando Valley. This house had four bedrooms and two baths so everyone could have their own bedroom.

At this time Bev was working for her father in his sash and door business in Pasadena. She would commute across the valley into Pasadena daily. With me teaching and the kids in school, Ed was alone all day, but in a comfortable environment. When Bev arrived back home from Pasadena, she would sit with Ed and chat—catching him up on the day's activities.

Ed's health continued to deteriorate and eventually he was on oxygen. He continued to go downhill until it became necessary for him to be put in a hospital. He moved from a hospital in Los Angeles to the Veterans Hospital in the Valley. Ed only lasted a couple of weeks there until he passed away. Bev gave him the same kind of love and care she had given Mabel.

Both of my parents ended up passing away in our home under the careful nursing and love of Beverly, and I have always cherished this relationship and memory of Bev's wonderful care of my parents.

Ed had a funeral plot in Mount Moriah Masonic Cemetery in Kansas City, so I took his body back there to be buried. In those days a person had to accompany a casket on a train across the country so I took the train with the casket alone to Moberly, Missouri. Shirley flew there and they had a nice funeral in Ed's home town where he lived for some thirty years. Mr. Bradley, an old farmer-type of guy was Ed's partner in the coal mine, and he was most kind and gracious to Shirley and me.

Chapter 7

Surviving the Depression

I was born in September 1923 and turned six in September 1929. Black Tuesday, on October 29, 1929, was a benchmark for the start of the Great Depression of the 1930s. The beginning of my life seemed to parallel the first ten years of the depression. My parent's divorce in 1928 put us on the bottom financial rung of society's ladder at that time. We never went hungry thanks to Uncle Jack, but we just didn't have any money available for personal purchases.

From a very early age I knew that if I wanted anything beyond the necessities of life I would have to earn it by myself. I was aware of the value of money and was not afraid to earn it penny by penny.

The first "working" job I had, and I got it by myself, was selling *Liberty* magazines door-to-door. They were a weekly magazine and cost a nickel. First I had to go door-to-door soliciting customers and then serviced them weekly. From the 5¢ per copy, I got to keep 2½¢ as my profit. I paid the man who brought the magazines to me the other 2½¢. Can you imagine a grown man driving around in a car delivering magazines to little boys for 2½¢ a copy? He couldn't have been making much money, and maybe he didn't get to keep the entire 2½¢, but that was the Depression in 1931 and he was probably glad to have any kind of a job.

I was about seven or eight years old at the time. I had a canvas sack that I slung over my shoulder to hold the magazines and I sold about ten *Liberties* a week, which earned me 25¢ a week.

In addition, once a month a movie magazine came out, the *Silver Screen* or something like that. It cost 35¢ an issue and I made 15¢ profit for them. I sold two or three a month so that was really big money! Movie people who were not on a regular salary, but only got paid when they worked, were notoriously slow in paying their bills. One or two people would take a screen magazine from me but wouldn't pay for it and put it on credit 'til next month. As I had to pay cash when I got the magazines, this really put a crimp in my cash flow. I don't believe anyone ever stiffed me for an entire magazine, but if someone owed me 70¢ for two months, this was really a reason for worry. I guess I learned the value of a penny or two, rules of business, and money management from this experience at the tender age of seven. I have probably been frugal and a tightwad all of my life from this early exposure to the marketplace.

When I was nine or ten I used to do yard work for 10¢ an hour and I worked long and hard at this wage, but I was glad to have the work at the time.

I remember working very hard for one woman. In addition to yard work I was cleaning out all of her gutters, which were full of eucalyptus leaves. It was really a hard, filthy job. I had put in seven to ten hours and she must have owed me a dollar but she wouldn't pay me. She would say, "Come back tomorrow afternoon and clean some more gutters." I worked hard for my 10¢ and I expected to be paid. I was really frustrated and asked my mother to go over to her house with me to get the woman to pay me what she owed. My mom was a very meek and passive person and I'm sure she didn't enjoy this, but she went with me to back me up. I did get paid what I was owed and then I quit and never worked for that woman again.

When I was twelve or thirteen I was in the Boy Scouts and had a chance to go on a one-week trip to Yosemite during the summer. The cost was $15 and I knew about the trip well in advance so I worked for every penny of my fee at 10¢ an hours. That amounted to 150 hours of work, or nearly a month of forty-hour weeks.

When I was in high school, my football coach got me a job driving a laundry truck for 35¢ an hour and I was really happy with that. I earned enough to go to college the following year.

Even when I had a degree and was a teacher, I held side jobs to help support my growing family. I have done just about everything. Some of the jobs I have had include the following: postman, policeman, longshoreman, tax preparer, lifeguard, truck driver, security guard in an atomic plant, naval officer, laborer, square dance caller, football referee, professional football player, camp counselor, convenience store clerk, office clerk, actor, and National Park ranger. I have probably forgotten several, but will say more about this later.

Working for pennies during the depression must have had a profound influence on my attitude about work—earning money, and building a savings throughout my entire life. I have had a good life, have been upwardly mobile in society, and have continuously gotten ahead. I have been retired for thirty-three years now and have a limited pension because I retired early. Due to some fortunate investments and living quite frugally, we have more money than we have ever had in our life. We did our income tax in the last couple weeks and our adjusted gross income is the highest it has ever been. Besides, I don't have any *Liberty* magazines I need to sell!

Chapter 8

The Movies

Uncle Jack, who supported my mother, my sister, and me during the Depression, had a famous dog in the movies in the 1920s and 1930s. Jiggs, the dog, played the mascot of the star in *Wings,* the first movie to ever win an Oscar as Best Picture of the Year at the very first Academy Award ceremony in 1928.

Because of Jiggs, Uncle Jack had access to all of the movie studios in Hollywood. When I was five years old in 1928, the family decided I should be in the movies. I don't know what the main motivation for this decision was, as I certainly didn't have any talent for acting. At that tender age, I didn't have any input in the discussion. I would say the main motivation was money. Mother and I didn't have any income of our own at the time. Mother didn't work other than doing the housework. I guess I was becoming the breadwinner for our family at the tender age of five. The pay for an "extra" or mob scene player in those days was $5 a day and my mother and I could certainly use the money. That was pretty fair wages for 1928. Five dollars was a lot to us when we didn't have any money coming in.

I remember my first movie was *Sidewalks of New York* starring Buster Keaton. It was one of the early "talkies." We worked several days shooting a big neighborhood riot or fight on a New York street scene.

Uncle Jack took me to the studio on his days off from the fire station. When he had to work, my mother took me. We went on the street car all the way out to MGM in Culver City. Mother and Jack would hide in the doorways and behind the fake walls while they were shooting a scene.

Jack took dirt from the ground and rubbed it on my face as makeup for realism, but it didn't make much difference in a mob scene of 100 men and boys having fistfights and throwing vegetables at each other. I don't think there were many women or girls in the riot scene.

From that humble beginning I was an extra in quite a few movies until I was nineteen years old and enlisted in the Marine Corps in 1942. I was always rather self-conscious and had no talent or interest in acting at all. Jack tried to have me memorize some poems and "pieces," but I even had trouble memorizing the lines, let alone reciting them with any dramatic flare. I did go to a casting call for *Skippy* around 1932, but Jackie Cooper got the part and became a big star after his first movie. I heard that he was the nephew of the producer and it was fixed, so I never had a chance.

I did have a few close-ups and shots where you could at least identify me in a scene, and occasionally I can spot myself on a late, late, old, old movie on TV.

In one film I was seated at the head table in the dining hall of a boy's school near the star, Freddy Bartholomew, in *John Brown's School Days*. I was standing at the shoulder of Bing Crosby as an orphan while he was singing the title song in *Pennies from Heaven*. The five or six of us huddled close around him were called the "Crosby boys" when they called us back after a break.

Even though I was young when I started, I was aware that I was "in" the movies. It was always a treat to get away from school for a few days, see some of the stars close up, and work with them, even in a very minor way.

Children of school age had to go to school several hours a day when they had time off between scenes. There is a lot of waiting around time when shooting a movie. You could bring your school-

books from home and take advantage of the certified teacher on duty to help you with your studies and homework. One day I was in class with Mickey Rooney and Judy Garland at MGM. We were all teenagers at the time. I was working on *Boy's Town* with Mickey and Judy was doing one of her first musicals.

In one scene in *Boy's Town* I was shoveling snow in the background. I was an orphan again, while Spencer Tracy, as Father Flanagan, was trying to get the Jewish moneylender, Lee J. Cobb, to give him a loan to keep Boy's Town afloat.

I was in *The Bride of Frankenstein* where Boris Karloff played Dr. Frankenstein's monster. My acting job was to run away from the monster, along with thirty other citizens on a dark and stormy night as he charged after us down the road. Mr. Karloff's costume weighed about forty pounds, which made him unable to sit down all day long. They provided an eight-foot-high tilted plank for him to lean up against. It included a four-inch wide shelf he could rest his butt on to take some of the weight off his legs to give him a break.

One evening around quitting time, I was standing about five feet from him while he was leaning up against his resting spot. As an assistant director approached, Mr. Karloff asked, "Is that all for today?" The director replied, "Yes sir, that's for sure." Mr. Karloff reached up and peeled off an inch-and-a-half-long, quarter-inch-thick piece of putty from his upper eyelid and flipped it to the ground beside my feet. He was glad to get rid of that impediment after a long day, and it was quite an exciting experience for a ten-year-old boy standing that close to the monster!

I was in college by the time I did my last movie. I think several of us got the job through the college. I had already enlisted in the Marine Corps and here I was playing a Nazi soldier going through a burning Russian village with a gun and a bayonet. By coincidence, I was reading the book *Mission to Moscow* at that time and had it on the set with me that day. I believe the movie was called *The North Star* and starred Anne Baxter, Walter Huston, and Walter Brennan. It was nominated for six Oscars.

Being in the movies was a fun experience and I could always use the extra money. None of my "acting" talent was passed along to anyone else in the family except for one granddaughter, Kendra. In her first outing she starred as Anne in *Anne of Green Gables* on the stage and she was good. It is interesting that the family never tried to exploit my sister Shirley in the movies like they did me.

Chapter 9

My First Bike

I grew up in the Depression. Of course, money was short and we made do with what ingenuity and imagination could create with what was at hand. I remember my first two-wheel bike was one my uncle Jack had made from a tricycle. It had a large wheel in the front and a small wheel behind, like the early bikes in the 1890s. It was only the size of a tricycle … but it was a two-wheeler! I outgrew that bike and for many years didn't have any bike. I used "shank's mare" to get where I was going and walked and hiked for miles from my home. One time I walked clear over to the famous Hollywood sign and climbed it to the top.

I don't remember how old I was, probably around ten or eleven, but it was Christmas Eve. We had a large front window where we always set up our Christmas tree so the lights would shine out to the street. It was already dark when I went out to get the evening paper. As I dashed out the front door (a ten-year-old boy never walks), there, sitting up on its kickstand on the front porch, was a brand new, real, shiny, full-size, two-wheel bike. I came to a screeching halt, my mouth flew open; I was in complete awe. There stood the most amazing thing I had ever seen, a gorgeous bike. It was the greatest Christmas present I ever got. My usual presents were underwear and socks and things I needed and perhaps one small toy or game.

I picked up the paper and went back in the house without saying a word. I didn't want to spoil their surprise. After dinner we opened our presents and had our usual humdrum Christmas Eve. I guess I should have busted in when I first saw the bike. As it was, the folks had to keep hinting to get me to look out the window until I could spot the bike. Then, all hell broke loose as the whole family erupted, sharing my joy. It was the best Christmas present I ever had until my third granddaughter was born at home on an early Christmas morning.

Of course, the bike was not a new one. My uncle Jack was a Los Angeles City fireman and he had found an old chassis and rebuilt it from the ground up while on duty at the fire station. It was the most beautiful bike I had ever seen.

Chapter 10

Uncle Jack

Uncle Jack was a most unusual man who led a very exotic life. He had a profound influence on my life for both good and bad. He was a native Californian, born in Los Angeles. I don't think he ever graduated from high school. He was a dough-boy in France in WWI at around sixteen or eighteen years of age. Following that, he was a lifeguard on the beach at Long Beach. He joined the Los Angeles City Fire Department, where he put in twenty years before retiring. His highest rank was auto-fireman, where he drove the front end of the old-fashioned ladder truck. The fireman steering the rear end was called the tillerman.

Uncle Jack had a pet dog named Jiggs which he took to the fire station with him on every shift. He trained the dog to do all kinds of tricks. Jiggs could say "mama" and "hamburger." I think he understood everything Uncle Jack said to him. Jiggs was a Boston bull terrier who had his ears cut to points when he was a puppy. He was a trim, medium-sized short hair dog. His coloring was rich brown with a few white spots here and there.

Jiggs became a movie star at MGM. At the height of the Depression in 1927–1930 he made $2,700 a week. The first Academy Award best picture of the year in 1927 was *Wings* and Jiggs played the mascot of the hero in that movie.

In WWII Uncle Jack's brother, Ross, was fire chief at Hickham Field on Oahu. He was there on Pearl Harbor Day and a Japanese bullet went into his bedstead in his quarters at Hickham Air Base.

During the war, Uncle Jack went over to Hawaii and became fire chief at Wheeler Field, which was by Schofield Army Base. After the war, he continued as fire chief at various military bases until his second retirement after twenty more years.

In spite of leading the exciting life described above, Uncle Jack was the most henpecked man I have ever known.

My mother, Mabel, had one sibling—her sister Julia—who was younger. Julia went to California on a vacation in the 1920s. Somehow she met Jack and they became a "thing." My grandmother, Amy Jadwin, was a very strong-willed person and the matriarch of the family. Grandpa Jadwin was a Kansas City police captain, but he died early in the '20s. Grandma moved to California to live with Julia. My mother, sister and I moved to California to live with Aunt Julia and Grandma after my parents divorced. We all lived in one happy household in the heart of the Depression with Uncle Jack paying the rent.

I don't know the details too specifically, or whether Jack and Julia were living together before they were married, but I remember going on their honeymoon with them. That is a famous family story that has been passed down through the years. They went to a little motel or group of cabins right on the beach sand around Santa Monica or maybe Malibu. Jack and Julia did have their own cabin, but Grandma, Mabel, Shirley and I were right next door in the next cabin. That was the beginning of Julia's dominance over Jack.

I grew up recognizing this relationship and living with it daily. In later years, Julia, who was perfectly healthy, would say, "Jack, light my cigarette," and he would get up from across the room to do it. She would say, "Jack, let the dogs out," then fifteen minutes later she would say, "Jack, let the dogs in," and he would get up from whatever he was doing and do so.

In his later years, Uncle Jack had a habit of saying to the grandchildren, "I'm a very remarkable fellow." He was that, but it was a pity that he had to say it about himself. There is much more that could be said about Uncle Jack and particularly about the effect his image had on me, but that will make another story. Actually, his character would make a pretty interesting book in itself.

Jack had the usual array of tools in the garage and was a pretty good "fix-it man." He could build a pretty good birdhouse, or repair a broken chair. I spent many hours of my childhood standing out in the garage watching him work. He would never let me touch the tools or build anything myself. This became boring—boring to me as I stood around for hundreds of hours of my life just watching him. I feel that this boredom gave me a real phobia against using tools or repairing things. I have carried this feeling with me all of my life. I am a very un-mechanical person as a result. If a light bulb needs changing in a lamp around our house, that is Bev's job, not mine. This is a real character flaw that I have from Uncle Jack.

Uncle Jack Ewing and Jiggs both have a scar for a movie shoot.

Chapter 11

Jiggs

Not everyone has the opportunity to grow up with a movie star in the house. I was one of the exceptions.

After our parents were divorced my mother, sister and I came to California to live with Mother's sister, Aunt Julia. Aunt Julia, had married Jack Ewing, a native of Los Angeles, and they lived in Hollywood. In those days families took care of their own. There wasn't as much welfare as there is today. Mother, my sister Shirley, and I moved in with Jack and Julia and Grandmother too, in Hollywood, where Jack was the breadwinner. When there was some downtime at the fire station where Jack worked, he would spend the time training his dog to respond to him. It was a one-man dog situation and Jack and Jiggs understood each other perfectly.

Somehow Jack got the dog into the movies and he became a star at MGM. He was as big a star in his time as Rin Tin Tin was, but his name was not passed down through movie history as well. Another popular dog was Petey from the *Our Gang* comedies, the one with a black circle painted around his eye.

Jiggs was a star for several years. In one movie, *The Love Parade* (1929) with Jeanette McDonald and Maurice Chevalier, Jeanette played a snooty rich girl and Maurice was a common man of the street who fell in love with her. There was a parallel story line in the movie between her dog, a French poodle, and our dog, Jiggs, a common mutt.

At one point MGM made a series of shorts or one-reeler movies in which all parts were played by dogs and parodied famous movies. *Trader Horn* was a famous movie about an African safari starring Harry Carey Sr. Jiggs was then in an all dog short film called *Trader Hound*. He was in many others as well.

Jiggs, the movie star at MGM. Photo by Bruno who did all the famous stars like Marilyn Monroe.

When making *Trader Hound* they had a stunt where Jiggs was wired to the back of a simulated lion. In the process of the stunt Jiggs fell off and ruptured himself. As a result, he died and that was that. Those days were long before the current climate of litigation, attorneys, lawsuits and massive compensation.

Jack and Jiggs were a unique combination and Jack never had another successful dog. He did not have a kennel full of dogs like the fifty or so I understand have played Lassie over the years.

Jiggs was never stuck up and gave his autograph (paw print) to anyone who asked. It was fun as a ten-year-old kid growing up in a house with a movie star.

Bruno of Hollywood was the most famous glamour photographer of the 1930s. He has done many famous stars of the time so he was chosen to do photos of Jiggs too. The portrait above of Jiggs was done by Bruno.

Chapter 12

Aunt Julia

Aunt Julia was very interesting to me in my growing-up years. She was the most dominant figure in our family while I was being raised.

My mother, Mabel, was a couple of years older than Julia and they were the only children of Amy Frazier Jadwin and Grandpa Jadwin, a police captain on the Kansas City, Missouri, force.

I don't remember many family stories from their childhood except for one. When they were girls, Julia hit Mabel in the head with a brick. I guess that set the pattern for the rest of their lives. Julia was dominant and Mabel was the docile one.

Julia was married early on in Kansas City but that was one of the family skeletons we kept in the closet. It was never discussed and I don't know whether it was annulled or if they were divorced.

Julia was not especially attractive, just an average-looking woman. As I remember, she didn't especially like to have her picture taken and we don't have many pictures of her around today.

Mabel didn't finish high school, but went to work around 1918. I don't know whether Julia finished high school or not, but she went to work early as a secretary or clerk. Mabel also did clerical work in a creamery. That is what they called milk processing plants in those days.

Julia went to California on a vacation in the early

1920s where she met and married Jack Ewing, a Los Angeles City fireman.

Grandma Jadwin was a strong-willed widow by that time and she moved to California to live with Jack and Julia.

My mother was divorced in 1928 and had nowhere to go so she and her two children, Shirley and I, moved in with Jack, Julia and Grandma. That is the ménage in which I grew up.

I don't know what wiles Julia had going for her, but she totally dominated Jack and the entire household. She was the queen bee and Mother was the maid. Julia was always the strong and able-bodied woman, but did very little around the house and was always waited on. Mother earned her keep and that of her children by doing all of the housework and cooking for the household. This gave us three meals a day and a place to sleep.

Jack and Julia had their bedroom, Grandma had a room, and Mother, Shirley and I shared a room with two beds. Mother and Shirley slept together and I had my own bed in the same room. There was a bath and a half for the household.

Somewhere along the line Julia developed cataracts and had them removed one at a time. In those days you were kept in bed for about a week with sandbags around your head so you couldn't move at all and then you had to be very quiet for several weeks of recovery with no bending or lifting.

The family always had dogs around. Jack had his dog, Jiggs, and Julia had her dog, Jerry. We lived in the Hollywood hills where there were empty lots and open undeveloped country around the houses. These lots were filled with ground squirrels. It was pretty easy to catch the squirrels alive in box traps. We then released the squirrels with the dogs standing by. They chased the squirrel until they caught and killed it. The squirrels never had a chance. This was a great spectacle for a twelve-year-old kid to observe. The dogs were Boston bull terriers and they went after the squirrels violently and viciously chewed them up. The dogs were highly agitated and in fierce competition with each other. So, after several squirrel encounters, the dogs got so they would fight aggressively whenever they met.

From that time on the dogs had to be separated. One became the house dog and the other had a kennel, doghouse, and run outside. Every time they would accidentally get together they would get into a dogfight.

While Julia was recuperating from her second cataract operation, the dogs got into a fight and she, without thinking, reached down to grab her dog and in so doing, ruptured the cataract incision. This made her sight less than perfect in one eye, and she used this, her only infirmity, to her advantage for the rest of her life.

Jack and Julia drank all of their lives and at some point were probably alcoholics. Jack reminds one of the general in the comic strip *Beetle Bailey* drawn by Mort Walker. The general is henpecked by his wife and is always drinking at the officer's club. Incidentally, Mort Walker is a fraternity brother of mine.

In his later years, Jack was fire chief at the Yuma Test Station and the U.S. Naval Ordinance Station near Ridgecrest, California, where he was definitely an alcoholic. At some point late in her life Julia did quit drinking entirely. Jack smoked and drank until his death from lung cancer after having one lung removed.

Julia outlived Jack by many years and lived alone in an apartment until her death. My sister Shirley was her primary caregiver although Julia lived independently. Neither Julia nor Mabel ever learned to drive a car.

One time my wife, Bev, and I were going on a backpack trip into the remote High Sierra. Julia asked how we could be reached there and I rather abruptly said there was no way that we could be reached. She may have had a premonition at that time. We were two days into the backcountry when a hiker came into our camp around dusk and asked if we were the Carter party. I answered, "Yes." He gave me a note from a forest ranger that said Aunt Julia had passed away.

Our daughter, Deanna, grown at the time, is a pretty smart girl and had been backpacking with us plenty in the past. She knew the general area and canyon we were planning to be in. She contacted the forest service and got the message to a backcountry ranger who sent the note on to us by a casual camper who was heading up the canyon on its single trail, where he came upon our bivouac.

It was too late to start that night, but the next morning with an early start, we hiked out a two-day journey in one day. It was maybe twenty or twenty-five miles, which was a lot for us with heavy packs. It nearly killed my wife, Beverly, and she developed some kidney or bladder problems as a result. After hiking all day we drove home to Southern California and arrived just in time for the funeral the next day. Julia, Jack and Mabel are side by side in the mausoleum in the Hollywood cemetery .

Chapter 13

The Library

When I was in the sixth or seventh grade I got my first real bicycle. That's when I discovered the big public library in downtown Hollywood about ten miles from our home up in the hills. Every Thursday I rode my bike down to the library and checked out five books, the maximum you could check out at one time. I then pedaled my bike back uphill all the way home. I read about a book a day and took all five back the following Thursday to get five more. I must have read 300 or more books a year when I was eleven or twelve years old. That contributed to a lifetime appreciation for reading.

I have always been a good reader and enjoy reading for fun and for knowledge. I'm sure this has helped me with my education all of my life. Now that I am in my eighties, I still read a book every three or four days.

We lived up the hill from Hollywood all the way over Cahuenga Pass, which was a two-lane street at that time, and is now the 101 Freeway going toward San Francisco. I rode my bicycle back and forth to school all through junior high school and until I was able to get my first car.

Early on I learned a clever trick that helped me in getting up the hill on my one-speed bicycle. In those days the cement and gravel trucks traveled about five miles per hour up the steep grade over Cahuenga

Pass. I could pedal as fast as they were traveling and grab hold of a chain on the back of the trucks. This chain was used to unhitch their tailgate to unload. I hung on just behind the rear wheels of the truck and let it pull me a couple of miles to the top of the pass near where I lived. The truck drivers saw me from their rear view mirrors, but they didn't seem to mind. They never dissuaded me in any way either by gestures or by stopping the truck to dislodge me. It was a free ride uphill that I used for many years with library books in my bag and all.

I started collecting stamps when I was ten years old and have been a collector and meticulous person about counting things and keeping records all of my life. I was out in the Pacific on a tanker for two years in World War II. Books were floating around on every ship out there and we traded books with each other all the time. I kept a list of all the books I read during the Navy. I read everything and anything I could get my hands on which included novels and fiction, philosophy, history, biography, science fiction, anything at all. I have long since lost that list, but I did bring it home with me and I know I read hundreds of books during those two years.

Chapter 14

Going to Junior High School

When I was twelve years old and in the sixth grade at Valley View School, a part of the Los Angeles school system, I went to a small, isolated, two-room school in the hills of Hollywood. The fourth, fifth, and sixth grades were all in one room and we had six students in the sixth grade.

The Los Angeles school district had a twice-a-year promotion system, held in February and in June. It seemed that Valley View wanted to have a February graduating class. In October, the teacher called Rose, Marilyn, and me aside and told us that we were going to graduate in February instead of June. We had just been skipped a half a grade ahead. I guess that we three had the highest test scores or were the three smartest kids out of the six in the sixth grade. The teacher gave us some extra books to study on our own time so we would be ready for junior high. I was the only boy in my graduating class of three.

In hindsight, this was one of the worst things that could have happened to me in education. At age twelve, girls are ahead of boys physically, academically, and socially. I considered myself a very average student and I was not getting straight A report cards. I was an athletic leader among the forty children in my elementary school, but I was pretty average in a group of 1,500 junior high students. Being in the February, mid-year class put me out of step with the rest of the sixth graders.

On the first day of junior high, I rode the big red streetcar into downtown Hollywood to Bancroft Junior High. I went into the large auditorium and sat down with three or four hundred seventh graders. I didn't know anyone else. Rose and Marilyn went on to a different junior high so I was all alone and twelve years old. I took my lunch in a brown paper bag and really felt like a small country boy in the big city.

They began to call kids up to the front of the room alphabetically by school. The big city schools had one or two sixth grade classes. When they called Adams school, thirty or forty kids went to the front. Then Cahuenga School was called and sixty kids went forward to get assigned to their classes. Pretty soon there was only one kid sitting alone in the big auditorium. Me! My school, Valley View was the last alphabetically and I was the only one left in the room. I felt pretty lost and lonely. I had been sitting there for two hours, had to go to the bathroom, and didn't even know where it was. What a predicament!

Chapter 15

Run Away

By the time I was fourteen, I realized that we had a pretty uncomfortable home life. My mother, my sister Shirley, and I didn't have any of our own money. We had been living by the grace of Aunt Julia and Uncle Jack on his Los Angeles fireman's salary for nine years and nothing was changing our status.

One evening Shirley had been invited to a party by a girlfriend who lived right behind us. The house was high on a hill so I could hear every word they said as they played outside. I hadn't been invited.

I guess I was pretty unhappy with our living arrangement. As I sat out in the backyard and listened to all of the happy activities going on right behind me, things just piled up and I felt overwhelmed.

I had been hitchhiking back and forth to school and to downtown Hollywood for several years, and was quite comfortable with that kind of transportation. Sitting there listening to all the sounds of the party, on the spur of the moment I decided to take off. I hadn't made any plans beforehand. I didn't take, or steal, any money from the house. I didn't even take a sweater or jacket with me. I just took off with only the shirt on my back. I had less than twenty-five cents in my pocket.

I walked the couple of blocks down to the nearest corner of the main highway, which is now 101. I was on my way to see Aunt Alice and Uncle Virgil Anderson in San Francisco. Aunt Alice was Uncle Jack's sister.

I stuck out my thumb and soon had a ride going north. I had a couple of short rides and then a couple of guys in a Model A Ford convertible with a canvas top picked me up. Three of us crammed into the front seat of the Ford. They were out on a "toot" and had been drinking. They had a gallon bottle of wine with them that was mostly gone. They offered me a drink. I had never had anything alcoholic to drink before, but not wanting to seem unfriendly, I took a snort or two. We arrived in the town of Ventura, about seventy miles from Hollywood. The main highway ran through the middle of town and became a regular two-lane city street with homes and businesses on either side.

The atmosphere was most friendly and all was going smoothly, but I could tell that the two guys were pretty drunk. It was now about ten P.M. and there wasn't much traffic on the streets of Ventura. Suddenly, for no apparent reason, the driver made a radical ninety-degree left turn right in the middle of the block. This turned the car over and we rolled a couple of times ending up on the front lawn of a house. We were upside down with all four wheels in the air and nothing between us and the ground except the canvas top of the convertible. As we were wedged in the front seat tightly, and the doors didn't come open, we were still side-by-side in the seat with our heads touching the ground.

Since I was on the outside, one of them said to me, "Open the door," so I did and climbed out of the wreck. Fortunately none of us was hurt very much. I had a few scratches on my back. We stumbled around the yard and I gathered my senses as a crowd began to form around us.

Eventually a police car arrived. Now, these fellows didn't know who I was, and I didn't know them, but I knew I didn't want to be involved with anything to do with this wreck. Besides, this incident was interfering with my goal of getting to San Francisco.

I just wandered away from the crowd and walked on up the street a block or two and started hitchhiking again. As all of the traffic had slowed down to look at the wreck, they were going very slow, so it was easy to get another ride right away. I left the scene very little the worse for wear.

I got several more rides through the night, but it was pretty slow and quiet just beyond Paso Robles, and I was stranded for a couple of hours at about three A.M. Finally I did get a long lift and did some sleeping along the way.

I arrived in San Francisco about noon, so I had made the entire trip in about sixteen hours of hitching. I hadn't had sense enough to even get Aunt Alice's name, address, or telephone number as I hadn't done any planning for this expedition. I guess I learned something from this experience and I believe all of my future trips had a much better agenda than this first reckless, impulsive trek.

Later, hindsight brought some better choices to my mind. I made one huge mistake. I passed several fire stations as I wandered around the San Francisco streets. I should have gone into the first fire station I saw and pleaded with them for help based on my relationship with three uncles whose occupation was with the Los Angeles Fire Department. I know they would have given me a meal and a little sound advice on how to proceed. They might even have let me sleep in the firehouse overnight. I had previously slept in Los Angeles firehouses several times with Uncle Jack when I was a youngster. He would have taken me on a fire run, too, had they had a call that night.

There were public phone booths on nearly every corner. There were many Andersons in the phone book as it is a fairly common name. I would pick an Anderson and ask questions of people on the street how to get to that address. When I arrived at an address I would then ask them if they knew Aunt Alice. This was a pretty inefficient way of going about my search. I hit dead ends all afternoon and wasn't getting anywhere at all. I hadn't eaten anything all day. I wasn't starving, but I was pretty hungry. That's when I made my third big mistake. My first big mistake was coming all the way to San Francisco without thinking it out and making some plans. My second mistake was not going into the first fire station I spotted. Now, instead of going to a fireman, I went to a policeman and told him I was hungry and asked where I could get something to eat. Big mistake! He took me to the nearest police station where they processed me through all the red tape and took me to Juvenile Hall where they threw me in the slammer. It was a single room with a small window in the door.

I hadn't said much to anybody as we went through all of this police business. I just went along with the flow. By this time it was about eight P.M. and I had missed dinnertime at Juvenile Hall, and I was hungrier than ever. When I realized that I was in isolation for the night I started screaming and pounding on the door until I got some attention. I told them that I hadn't eaten all day, had missed their dinnertime, and that the only reason I was there was because I was hungry. They did rustle me up some grub and I finally got a square meal that day.

My mom had reported me missing to the police. The family thought I was probably heading for Missouri to see my dad. The cops ID'd me from the clothes I had on based on the police report from Los Angeles. They kept me in solitary for a couple of days until they could finish the paperwork, then a plain-clothes detective or social worker took me down to the train station and put me on a train back to Los Angeles. I could have gotten off at any stop along the way, but I had had enough excitement for one excursion so I was glad to head for home.

Uncle Jack counseled with me when I got home and the point of his evaluation seemed to be that I had made my declaration of independence from that family situation at the tender age of fourteen. Since he was one of the most henpecked men I ever knew, I think he wished that he had gone with me.

Chapter 16

On the Farm

As a result of my runaway to San Francisco, my family felt that I wanted to leave home if I could and that hard work wouldn't hurt me. Our family had attended a small church in Hollywood called Unity. The pastors were a husband and wife team, Bob and Loretta Saunders. We had attended their church for about four years and had become very close to them. They had given up the church and retired to a farm in Chino, California. Loretta had developed cancer so Bob worked the farm and took care of Loretta as she faded away. Our family had kept in touch with the Saunders through all their difficulties and we were still close to them. My family had shared my problems with them and arranged for me to go and work on their farm when school was out in June.

I didn't see any problem with this arrangement, so I readily agreed to it. When school was out, the family drove me out to Chino and dropped me off for the summer. I slept outside on the front porch on a cot and took my meals with Bob and Loretta. There were just the three of us living in the house. Bob had a Mexican family who all came to work on the farm as they were needed. This included a father, mother, and children.

I had been doing yard work since I was ten years old so I was used to hard physical labor. I enjoyed the work and I was being paid a small wage plus room and board.

Bob had about an acre of gladiolas planted that he was growing for a cash crop at the wholesale flower market. One of my primary jobs was to get up every morning at 6:00 A.M. and walk through the gladiola patch cutting all of the flowers that were ready for market. As I cut them with a sharp knife, I would fan out a dozen in my hand at one time and then place them in boxes along the rows. When finished cutting, I carried the boxes to the truck and loaded them. Bob then took them off to market. That was my job every day before breakfast.

Bob had several other crops. He had a lot of corn that he grew for the nearby grocery stores in Chino and Pomona. I picked corn and carried the boxes from the field to the truck. I also cultivated the corn behind a horse-drawn plow. This was a new and interesting experience for me and one I caught onto quickly.

The Mexican family were all experienced good workers and very happy with their situation. I enjoyed working alongside them. Bob was the boss and all of the other workers on the farm were Mexican except for me. They accepted me easily and I learned a great deal about the Mexican culture and the status of farm workers from them.

Bob let me drive his pickup around the farm, so I learned to drive a stick shift that summer even though I didn't have a drivers license.

I remember one hot, dry windy day we had been working hard and I was completely covered with a thick film of dirt from head to toe. Normally I took a bath in their bathroom, but Loretta took one look at me and said, "He is not going to take a bath in my bathroom." Bob was an amazing, easygoing, levelheaded guy, and he was always very good to me. There were a couple of teenaged boys from the Mexican family still around and they were as dirty as I was. There was a stream or river near Chino so Bob said, "Vernon, why don't you take the truck and these two kids with you and go and take a bath in the river?" This sounded like a good idea to me, so I took off with the three of us in the cab. By this time it had turned dark, but off we went anyway. I didn't know for sure where the river was, but the other boys had an idea. We got lost a couple of times, but with their guidance we did find a pool deep enough for us to get into. We all took off our clothes and jumped naked into the pond where we got the dust and dirt off.

We found our way home without any further casualties and I went to the dinner table reasonably clean with smiles all around since I hadn't sullied Loretta's bathtub.

Chapter 17

Report Card

When I was sixteen years old and a junior at Hollywood High School, I was a good football player, although still pretty small in stature. They had an exponent system based on age, height, and weight. Since I had been skipped a half grade in the sixth grade I was quite young compared to the others in my class. I was only rated a B in my junior year, though I was considered a star and was the biggest, toughest kid on the B team. I got tattooed when I was fourteen so was a pretty rough looking character in the locker room. As the biggest player on a small team, I played left tackle on offense and defense which was the most difficult position as the point of attack in the ancient days of the single-wing formation. It was said in one game that I made three out of five of the tackles by the whole team. After that, one of my nicknames was "three out of five Carter."

I always enjoyed school, but was just a so-so student. I figured I was average and since C's were average that was okay with me. As I was getting a little older and more mature, better grades began to mean more to me. We carried our report cards around from class to class for the teachers to record our grades each period. I had a pretty heavy academic load including geometry, Spanish II, chemistry, English, and civics. On my final report card that semester I got an A in first period, another in second period and so on during the day. It was the first time in my life I had a straight A report for all six classes. PE was the last period of the day because of football. "Doc" Pash, our B football coach made a funny decision that day. He gave every member of the squad from the lowliest substitute to the star first stringers a B grade. There I was at the end of the day with my first straight A report card ever with a B in physical education. even though I was a first team star tackle.

Boy was I mad at the PE department. There was only one way to get out of PE and that was to join the ROTC. I joined the ROTC the next semester to avoid going back to gym and those PE teachers.

Aside from the incident related above, "Doc" Boris Pash was a pretty smart fellow and became a very important person in WWII. He was born in California of Russian parents. His father was a Russian Orthodox priest and the family returned to Russia in 1912. Boris had the nickname "Doc" at Hollywood High. I don't know why he assumed the name or its significance, but that is the name by which I knew him in school. I will continue to refer to him as "Doc," but his true name was Boris T. Pash. Doc graduated from seminary school in 1917 and returned to the United States in 1921. He became a reserve officer in the Army while teaching at Hollywood High.

Doc was called up to active duty in 1940. He was a security officer for the Manhattan Project in Los Alamos, and toward the end of the war he was the military leader of the Alsos Mission. Its purpose was to determine how far the Axis had progressed toward developing nuclear weapons, and to secure atomic materials and capture scientists working on the Nazi Atomic Project. Doc was ideal for this project since he spoke fluent Russian and, as I said, was a pretty smart fellow with a master's degree from USC and twenty years of teaching experience.

Doc wrote a book about his war experiences. It was titled *The Alsos Mission* by Boris T. Pash, Col., AUS Ret.(Award House, New York, 1969).

Colonel Pash is a member of the Military Intelligence Hall of Fame.

Chapter 18

B.M.O.C.

"BMOC" means Big Man on Campus. It was a common expression when I went to high school and also in college. It is probably still used today, but I haven't been on a high school or college campus for many years so I can't vouch for that from personal experience. It may be a long-dead expression for all I know, especially the way slang changes from decade to decade and from one part of the country to another. From what I hear on TV, today's kids only know three words, "like" and "ya' know."

A BMOC can apply to either a girl or a boy and is used referring to someone who stands out above the average student in one way or another. All of the star athletes in all sports were BMOCs as well as students who excelled in drama, music, or academics. The student body president, class presidents, and most members of the student council were certainly BMOCs. What it boiled down to was recognition. If a person was recognized by most members of the student body, even if they didn't know him personally, he was surely a BMOC

I guess I was a BMOC in both high school and college. My wife considered me a BMOC in college as I was president of the Associated Men Students and president of my fraternity twice, once before WWII, and again as a returning veteran after the war. I was on the student council and on the honor court. Occidental College operated on the honor system and "cheats" were handled by a jury of their peers—the honor court. This story is really about my high school experiences, though, and not college.

I earned my first athletic letter as manager of the baseball team in the tenth grade which earned me entrance into the Letterman's Club. I was also in the Hi Y, a club associated with the YMCA. I made the honor society one year, and one semester when I joined the ROTC, I won the Best Recruit medal.

In my senior year I was a star first-string guard on the varsity football team and was also elected a member of the student council. I guess all of the above qualified me, more or less, to be a BMOC as I was pretty well recognized and known by all of the students of our large 2,700-student Hollywood High School.

I graduated in the summer of 1941 so we are talking about the late 1930s, the end of the Great Depression and the beginning of WWII. Since my folks were divorced and we didn't have much money during the Depression years, I always considered myself one of the "poor" kids of Hollywood High and certainly of Occidental College when I attended there.

When our great president Franklin Delano Roosevelt was inaugurated he instituted many programs to help people through the Depression by giving them jobs and training. Most people are aware of many of those programs such as the Civilian Conservation Corps, Works Progress Administration, and Tennessee Valley Authority. One of those programs was called the CYA or California Youth Authority. It was a work program for needy students and I certainly qualified. I heard about that program somehow. Maybe it was posted on a bulletin board. I have always been a bulletin board reader. Maybe a counselor told me about it.

I was never shy or bashful about work or trying to get ahead so I applied for this program. I was obviously qualified as needy and willing to work so I was assigned to help the janitor, or custodian, as we called them in the schools. I helped him clean out the boys' gym in the mornings before school. My usual assignment was to sweep out all of the coaches' offices, empty their wastebaskets, dust, and in general clean up the place. I went to school about seven A.M. and spent an hour cleaning up. The coaches came drifting into work during that time. I was paid 25¢ to 35¢ an hour and spent a couple of my high school years doing this. The custodian and coaches knew I did this menial work, but I don't think any other person at school knew about it. Certainly no students were aware of it as I was finished before they arrived. I was very grateful and happy to get my 25¢ a day. When I was finished I would wander out on campus and join the rest of the students for fifteen or twenty minutes before class. I took off my "peon" hat and put on my BMOC hat. I was not ashamed that I was doing this kind of work, in fact, I was proud that I was earning my own way. I just felt that it was private and that the kids in school didn't need to know about it. It was definitely a well-kept secret. I've had many high school friends for over fifty years now and I don't believe that any of them know to this day that I cleaned out the gym before school every day.

I don't believe that it would have changed anyone's opinion of my BMOC status had they known about it. I know it wouldn't have made any difference with my close good friends like Phil, Rose, Shirley

Howard, Marilyn or Tak. Both the BMOC experience and sweeping out the gym were events that made my life richer and fuller and I have appreciated them all.

Chapter 19

Romeo

When I was in high school I considered myself average, an average student, and average in my social life. The only way I felt above average was as a football player. In my senior year I was a first-string guard on the varsity team, and one of the best of eleven football players out of a school of 2,700 students.

Los Angeles is a very large, spread out city and transportation is a big problem especially for teenagers who are beginning to date and go to places with girlfriends. I started out by double dating with a buddy who had a car. I remember double dating with my sister Shirley who was going with a friend of mine, Avery Chatham. He was a year or two older than I and owned a car before I did. Through Avery I met a girl from Los Angeles High School named Margaret Stringfield. Her father was a professor at USC and she lived quite a long way from the Hollywood area, but we made a trip over there to pick her up. She was a pretty hot number and I remember necking with her in the back seat. I didn't pay much attention to what my sister was doing in the front seat.

When I was in the eleventh grade I bought my first car. It was a 1931 Model A Ford. In 1940 it was nine years old and I paid $100 for it. I earned every penny for that car myself, mostly at 35¢ an hour. It was a pretty slick, hardtop coupe in very good condition. I was mighty proud of it. It did burn a little oil so my closest neighborhood buddy, Phil Haisley, and I put new rings in the four pistons to cut down on the oil consumption. Phil was the son of Colonel Haisley who was in charge of the ROTC program at Hollywood High. This was in 1940 before WWII started. Phil went to West Point and became a colonel himself before he retired thirty years later.

Another buddy I double dated with a lot was Howard Layne. We were the closest of friends all through high school and also went to Oxy together where we joined the same fraternity. We still keep in touch by phone three or four times a year. I remember one occasion when Howard's car had a weak battery that wouldn't start his car, so he always parked on a hill and I would get out of the car and push it until it picked up enough speed to turn the engine over. One time we were parked in a drive-in restaurant with a couple of girls. We were facing the restaurant with maybe five or ten feet of space to the sidewalk of the building. We were ready to go, but the carhop had not taken the trays from the car yet. It was a little downhill toward the drive-in. Howard let the car coast a couple of feet, then he popped the clutch which started the engine, then he slammed on the brakes before we hit the building. This worked out fine as the car started, but he had forgotten all the malted milk glasses and dishes on the trays and they flew off and all over the car. Fortunately no one got hurt, we didn't hit the drive-in, and we didn't even break any dishes, but it was a real mess. Ah youth!

When I had my own wheels I was able to ask girls out for a date and pick them up. This improved my social life greatly, and I dated lots of girls in high school.

During my junior year I started going steady

with Shirley Eames, a peach of a girl. I had known her for three years and had shared some classes with her and we were in the same homeroom together. She was one of the best looking girls in school and one of the sharpest. She was absolutely top quality, A1 in every category. I was amazed that she saw anything in me and that I was able to capture her interest. I guess we did make a good-looking couple and everyone knew that we were a twosome. We probably went together for nearly a year including summer vacation and had some wonderful trips to the beach in my Model A. But, as time went on, I felt that she was way out of my class and too good for me. I seemed to have an inner feeling that she was way above me and I didn't deserve such talent and good luck.

In those days we graduated in the Hollywood Bowl. We had two classes a year of about 500 students each. We all sat in the large shell over the stage where the operas were presented and where symphonic orchestras played. Our parents and friends sat in the open air on a hillside looking down onto the stage.

In the fall, Shirley was selected as valedictorian of her class and she would stand at the podium in front of her class in the Hollywood Bowl to give her speech. I remembered that I was from a divorced family. We didn't have much money. I was still sweeping out the gym and emptying waste baskets in the coaches' offices before school every morning and felt that I was in way over my head and not in her class.

The senior prom was coming up and it was assumed that Shirley and I would go together, but I was very depressed with the whole situation. One night, on the spur of the moment like the time I ran away from home, I called her on the phone and told her I thought we should break up and that I would not be taking her to the prom. I was the one who broke it off with the most outstanding girl in the school. Ah, young love!

I believe Shirley went to the prom with Bruce Gerry, a guy who was taller than I and better looking. After college they got married and have lived happily for some sixty years now.

Serendipity! When I was about forty years old, Bev and I ran into them at a ski area one day and had a chat with them over a sandwich and coke.

After Shirley left school in February, I began dating other girls for a while on a casual basis. Finally, I began to go steady with a girl named Isabel Ressler. She was Jewish, slightly on the chunky side, and not as good looking as Shirley, but a fine, sharp girl with a big smile and a great personality. We enjoyed each other's company very much and ended the school year graduating together from Hollywood High School in the summer of 1941 .

It just so happened that Isabel became valedictorian of our graduating class also. I may not have been much of a Don Juan or Casanova in high school, but I might have set an all American record by going steady with two class valedictorians, especially since I was a not too bright football player type.

Isabel and I had a good time all that summer until I started college, and then we just drifted apart. Isabel married a Jewish gentleman and I saw her a couple of times over the years at Hollywood High alumni gatherings. So much for a short story of high school puppy love.

Chapter 20

Occidental College

As I went through school I was just an average student. I enjoyed school, did my homework, never cut class, but considered myself as average. My mother never graduated from high school and no one from my family ever mentioned college or had any expectations for me beyond high school. I got better grades in my junior and senior years of high school and thought I would probably go down to Los Angeles City College and take some classes after graduation, as I could see that education was the tool that would open more doors for me in the future.

My high school football coach, Meb Schroeder, whom I admired and respected and was a great mentor for me, no doubt saw my test scores and knew that I was above average in IQ. He had graduated from Occidental College in Eagle Rock, which was just across town in LA from Hollywood. He took my best friend, Howard Layne, and me over to Oxy and introduced us to the football coach there. Howard and I were the right and left guards on our high school team. Howard's dad was a contractor and he had money behind him so I don't know about his financial arrangements, but Coach Schroeder arranged for me to get grants and aide to go to Oxy. This amounted to a football scholarship. Oxy was a prestigious, expensive college similar to USC and Stanford. It was not a government supported public school like UCLA.

Meb Schroeder was my high school football coach who was my idol and mentor. I wanted to be a coach just like him. Meb got me a football scholarship to Oxy.

After football season in my senior year of high school, Coach Schroeder got me a job driving a laundry truck after school and on Saturdays for another Hollywood High School alumnus. I got 35¢ an hour, which was pretty good money for a kid in 1941. If I worked three hours a day after school I would make $1.05 or about a dollar a day. Eight hours on Saturday would bring me $2.80, so I made about $8.00 a week. When school was out in June, I worked full-time all summer. I made enough, along with my grants in aide to go to Oxy in the fall. As I remember, the tuition was about $400 a year. That was a lot of money in those days. You could go to City College for about $10 and to UCLA for probably $50 or so.

I have always been proud of the fact that I earned my college education and degrees totally by myself, except for the help of some people like Coach Schroeder and my dad, who were my mentors along the way.

I know that there were other financially poor students at Oxy who received financial aid and scholarships, but I always felt that I was one of the poorest people to ever attend that prestigious institution.

I bought my first car, a used 10-year-old Model A Ford for $100 when I was fifteen or sixteen so I had my own wheels and I started college as a student commuting from home daily. This was the lowest rung in the social pecking order, as there were college dorms which cost $2,000 a year or so and private off-campus housing, as well as sorority and fraternity houses for all of those who were a part of the campus scene.

I started in September 1941, before WWII, and it was still a pretty naïve time with college traditions continuing from the '20s and '30s. For the first week or so there was freshman orientation accompanied by a little hazing. All freshmen wore gold beanies and big signs hung around their necks by a string with their names printed in large letters so everyone would get to know each other. The freshman class was about 400 students and the entire college had an enrollment of about 1,600. That tradition has long gone and I can't imagine high school grads today wearing a sign with their name on it.

I was a PE major and wanted to be a coach, just

like Mr. Schroeder, my idol. On my first day, I met Dr. Trieb who would be my mentor and nemesis for the next seven years. Oxy was very well organized and all classes were available without computer help, not like it is today. I took a full load: US history and British civilization, Spanish I, biology I, with a lab and some PE classes. I was also a starter on the football team. Roy Dennis was the freshman coach. He had gone to Oxy himself in the '30s and spent his life and career there. He was not a great coach but a wonderful man who took a sincere interest in all the college boys. Bill Anderson, the athletic director, was also a great guy who did anything he could to help the boys along. They were both very kind to me and helpful in many ways that I didn't realize at the time. They knew I was a poor kid and would give me many odd jobs around the gym so I could make some extra money.

Chapter 21

Housing at Oxy

I started college by living at home and commuting daily. This did not enable one to participate fully in campus activities. You missed out on a lot of things. After the first semester I joined the Kappa Sigma fraternity and I was able to move into the fraternity house for the next semester. There was a pecking order of priority in room assignments. Upper classmen had two-man rooms but the freshmen lived in one large room full of bunk beds on the back porch. Somewhere between ten and twenty men lived on the porch. Each man had only one closet or locker to store his clothes and belongings in. Of course, I worked my way up to a two-man room before I graduated and had several great roommates. One was a Navy pilot who stayed in the service after WWII and later was killed landing on an aircraft carrier. Another roomie became superintendent of the Long Beach School District. Both he and I got our doctorates and became superintendents of schools.

During the war, Oxy was taken over by the Navy and Marine Corps for the V-12 program, which was for officer training. I signed up for the draft while working in Las Vegas between my freshman and sophomore years. Then, when the draft board was after me, I enlisted in the Marine Corps for officer training. The Marines called me up for active duty on July 1, 1943, and sent me right back to Oxy in the

V-12 program in uniform. They took over the girls dormitories for the military, so then I lived in Oxy in a two-man room as a dormitory resident.

After the war, when I returned to Oxy, I lived in the fraternity house again. When we got married, my wife had graduated, but I still had a semester to go, so then we lived in a temporary Quonset hut-type building which was brought on campus for veteran housing. So, in my seven years at Oxy, I lived off campus, at home, in a fraternity house, on campus in a girls dormitory, and in veteran's housing.

President Barack Obama went to Oxy for two years before going east to school. He lived in a dorm named Haines Hall which is now of national fame, and his room is a historical landmark. My wife Beverly also lived in Haines Hall, some fifty years earlier. My V-12 dorm was named Orr Hall and is next door to Haines.

Since I am a Democrat, I was for Obama from very early in the race, and the Occidental connection made it doubly assured that he got two votes from this household. We wonder why anyone would want the job as president, and especially in these trying times, but we wish him the best as he tries to untangle this great but confused country of ours. We are justly proud that a former Oxy student is president of these United States.

Chapter 22

Kappa Sigma

Occidental College was blessed by having four strong national fraternities on campus. They were an important part of college life. I started college in 1941 and was living at home in Hollywood, commuting daily to Oxy in Eagle Rock, some twenty miles away.

Oxy had several large dormitories and they were very expensive—way over my head. Other students lived in fraternity and sorority houses that were less expensive. The lowest caste in this hierarchy would be students who lived at home and commuted to college. That was my position. Living at home, one missed the camaraderie of living with other students, participating in the evening bull sessions, and other extra-curricular activities such as football rallies, dances, casual get-togethers, etc.

One of the most important influences in my life from my college experiences was joining the Kappa Sigma Fraternity. Growing up without a father, or a strong male role model in my family, must have had a profound impact on my relationships with other people, and between men and women. I grew up sharing a bedroom with my mother and sister. A fraternity was a chance to live and share facilities with thirty other men my age.

Every year all of the Greek houses have a "rush" period to attract new members. Prospective members are invited to special lunches and dinners to look over the houses. This also provides an opportunity for the members to appraise the future pledges. It was an exciting time meeting new people, trying to impress them and them trying to impress you. I was a first-stringer on the freshman football team, and was invited to all four fraternities for lunch.

As they say in real estate, "location is everything." The KΣ house was on a corner right across the street from the main entrance to the college which was the best location of all.

The Phi Gams were on the opposite corner, also a favorable spot. The Ωs were located a block away, down the street on another corner.

I was invited to join all four fraternities. The Σ s were not a consideration as far as I was concerned. They were the most scholarly. The Phi Gams were a distant third on my rating scale. They were the more social and well-to-do college boys, which I was not. The ATO and KΣ houses were made up mostly of athletes and football players. This is where I could fit in. A number of my buddies on the football team, such as Dick Cooper, Ray Vernoy, Bill Scott, and Al Fain, pledged the Ω house. The KΣs went after me in a more forceful way. They welcomed me and told me that they wanted me. A couple of the senior members of the varsity team were in that house, George Jennings, the star back, and Burt Jones, a big, burly tackle. I decided to join the Kappa Sigs, which was one of the best decisions I ever made in my life.

There were about thirty or forty men in each fraternity. The KΣ house had six two-man rooms and a large porch across the back of the house. This porch area served as a dorm room for about ten men, with each man having a single big locker for his clothes.

The rent was quite reasonable compared with the college dorms. Not all members lived in the fraternity house. Some lived in the college dorms, and some had private apartments off campus.

I was looking for the most inexpensive way of living on campus so I moved into a bunk on the big back porch. I also learned that if you washed dishes you could get your meals free, so I became a dishwasher too.

The fraternity life opened up a whole new world for me. I got away from home for the first time in my life; I found a place to live on campus; and I had about forty "brothers" who became friends for life.

One of my closest friends, Jerry Peterson, passed away last year. Even today in 2009 another brother, Howard Layne and I still stay in touch by phone two or three times a year.

Hoagy Carmichael, who wrote *Stardust* and many other great songs, was a KΣ from the University of Indiana. He lived in Beverly Hills and was very friendly with our chapter at Oxy. During our rush week, Hoagy would come over to the KΣ house where he would sit around playing the piano and singing some of his well-known songs. This was pretty strong medicine for an impressionable seventeen-year-old kid. Later, Hoagy invited some of us to his house on several occasions to help him work on a Kappa Sigma songbook he was preparing for our national fraternity. When Hoagy passed away he was buried on the campus at Indiana University where he had written *Stardust* and enjoyed his college life as a Kappa Sig.

When I joined the KΣ house I was only seventeen years old, but I was paying my own way through college and was totally independent from that point on in my life.

We had a great cook named Anna, an old German lady who came in and cooked lunch and dinner for us. We were on our own for breakfast. A two- or three-man crew cleaned up and washed the dishes after the meals. As I was one of the neediest students attending Oxy, I was always on the lookout for jobs to help support myself. When there was an opening, I joined the dish crew and got all of my meals free for doing that chore. That cut down on my living expenses considerably.

When young people go to college they must learn how to deal with smoking, drinking, drugs, and sex to name a few important social ramifications of becoming an adult. I have never smoked, always joking that "I quit when I was ten years old." I came along before the drug problems of the '60s, so I was never faced with that problem or decision.

I drank a few beers while I was in high school. As I matured, I guess I passed for an adult by the time I was sixteen. I don't remember being asked for an ID for a drink after I reached age seventeen. The KΣs were reputed to be "boozers." There was a bar near campus called the Pago-Pago. The KΣs supported that bar and it was our private hangout. Of course I was introduced to the Pago by my fraternity brothers. I drank plenty from that time on in my life but, fortunately, I could hold my liquor very well and I didn't like to get drunk or lose control of my senses. I drank for social reasons with my buddies. If they needed someone to drive them home, I was usually selected even though I had been drinking as much as everyone else. I did go beyond my limit a few times, but I was never proud of that and probably held back some the next time.

Fraternities are often portrayed as elite, snobbish groups, but our house was very liberal and we prided ourselves on that attribute. At that time, of course, the national fraternity did not permit Negroes or Orientals. Jews, I think, were allowed. We at Oxy were all Caucasian, but prided ourselves on having Greek, Russian, and Mexican-born members. We were proud of our brothers named Xanthos, Komoroff, Perez, and Schmelzer. We also had a few Norwegians and Swedes, and at least one Communist.

Sammy Lee, a Korean, was the Gold Medal Olympic diving champion from Oxy. He was an outstanding human being, later becoming an ophthalmologist and Olympic diving coach. He was an all-around great guy. Sammy was a particularly good friend of the KΣs and we wanted to pledge him and have him become a "brother." As he was an Oriental, this was against the International KΣ rules. We had quite a scene over this, and many of the members were willing to be "kicked out" of the national fraternity by pledging Sammy. I won't say that "cooler heads" prevailed, but the decision was finally made *not* to pledge Sammy. I have always regretted that decision. I would be especially proud to have him as my brother.

Many years later after I left, my old house pledged a black man and they were expelled from the national fraternity as a result. Kappa sigma is very powerful in the South and originated at the University of Virginia where the southern influence has always been felt. I believe it is now allowed to pledge blacks and Orientals, so times do change for the better. I am writing this a couple of weeks after Barack Obama's election as our president-elect. I am proud that I was in a position to vote for the first black man for president of our country.

I entered Oxy in September 1941. Pearl Harbor

was December 7, 1941, so the men began to drop out of college to enter the services. In 1943, when I was just a sophomore, I became president or Grand Master of the fraternity since many of the older men had already gone off to war.

In the summer of '43, Johnny Logan and I lived in the fraternity house as "security and maintenance" men. We also worked as longshoremen in San Pedro and Long Beach. This was a great opportunity for us as there were not enough men left to load ships and the money was good. The work was scheduled on a twenty-four-hour day in two ten-hour shifts with an hour for lunch and an hour between shifts. We worked nights as the night shifts paid more and we could sleep in the quiet fraternity house all day. One night we loaded a ship from top to bottom with five-hundred-pound bombs. Another night we unloaded a full banana boat. I will never forget Harry Belafonte and his famous *Dayo* song—"Six foot, seven foot, eight foot stalks ..."

I returned from the war in 1946 and the KΣ house was back and functioning as a fraternity by that time. Since there was an opening, I moved right back into the house the same week that I was sworn out of the service. By this time I had worked my way up to a two-man room in the front of the house. We were made up mostly of returning veterans at that time and we had a very strong house.

In 1947 I was elected president or Grand Master of the house again, so I was president twice, during and after the war with a four-year separation in time. I am most proud of the fact that I was chosen twice by my brothers to be their leader. I have always cherished that memory and honor. We had quite a strong college political system at that time, and my fraternity brothers convinced me to run for AMS president. I was elected president of the Associated Men Students of the college that same year. I was, likewise, quite proud of that honor.

One of the protocols in the house was that members couldn't eat their meals until the president rang the bell and we had a prayer. I sat at the head of the table and ran the show, but after lunch, I was out in the kitchen again, washing dishes for my meals. I never in my life turned down a job when it was available or when I had a chance to make a few extra bucks. One can see how especially dear the fraternity was to me. It was my home for seven years, before, during, and after the war.

Kappa Sigma was always one of the top fraternities in America. I still receive their national magazine and find that in the year 2008 we are the number one fraternity in the country. We are the largest in terms of membership with the most chapters and the most pledges of any fraternity. Many great and famous men are my brothers.

Many years ago I had the pleasure of shaking hands with the governor of Texas, a brother. Our 2007 Man of the Year was a brother, Alan Mulally, president and CEO of the Ford Motor Company. Another famous Kappa Sig, Bob Dole, the senator from Kansas was our Man of the Year in 1970. I have already mentioned Hoagy Carmichael earlier in this chapter, the writer of *Stardust* as well as the popular song *Heart and Soul*. That song's chord progression became very common in doo-wop hits and is also known as the '50s progression.

My wife Beverly, was a member of the Zeta Tau Zeta Sorority. Her sorority house was conveniently located just around the block from the Kappa Sigma house. Our two chapters were particularly close to one another in many ways. We dated many Zetas and several of us married Zetas. My sister Shirley was also a Zeta and she and Beverly were the best of friends while I was out in the Pacific during the war. The first step in a romantic relationship to officially proclaim a union is when a frat man would give his "love" his fraternity pin, which she proudly wore. This was called "pinning." The entire fraternity traveled around the block and serenaded the girl and her sorority. The next step was an engagement ring. On this occasion the girl passed chocolates to announce to her sorority her engagement. This, of course, required another serenade.

My grandmother, Amy Jadwin, had a nice diamond known as "Grandma's diamond," that remained in the family after her death in 1941. I was given the diamond and had it made into an engagement ring for Beverly. In 1946 we were both living in our respective fraternity and sorority houses. I was still playing professional football at the time even though I was still a student at Oxy. Our team flew over to Hawaii to play two games with their professional team, the Hawaiian Warriors. My uncle Jack was fire chief at Wheeler Air Force Base at Schofield Barracks, so he and Aunt Julia were living there at that time. I took "Grandma's diamond" in Beverly's ring with me to show them before I presented it to Beverly.

Bev and I got married in June of 1947 and after a honeymoon trip through the Midwest to see all of our relatives, we returned to California. "Gunny" McDaniel, a gunnery sergeant in the Marine Corps in WWII was also a Kappa Sig. Gunny was my best man at our wedding and I was his best man the following

Vernon holds fraternity brother Vince Mattola. Note broken leg in a cast and beer bottles on the beach.

night. His wife was also a Zeta, as was my wife. After our honeymoon to Wisconsin and back, the four of us newlyweds drove all the way across the country again that same summer to attend the Kappa Sigma National convention that was held in Biloxi, Mississippi.

The Kappa Sigma experience was a very important one in my life, and I have been forever thankful for it. I have always had a feeling for belonging to organizations where I could do some good for others and make a contribution. I think I did for the KΣs.

Chapter 23

Oxy Freshman Year

I was a starter on the freshman football team. We had a couple of all-LA City guards on the team and I had played guard in high school. Coach Roy Dennis wanted his best eleven men on the field, so he made me a left end and I played first string on both offense and defense.

Sparkletts Water Bottling Company was just across the street from Oxy and it was a job source for years for Oxy students and particularly strong, needy football players. After football season was over I got a job there unloading water trucks at night. As they delivered the five-gallon bottles of water, they picked up the empty bottles, put them in the square wooden protective crate and put them back on the truck. The drivers put their trucks in a parking lot and checked in, doing their paperwork. When the night crew came on, we moved the trucks one at a time to the unloading dock. There we unloaded about 120 empties off each truck and put them on a track that rolled them away from the truck. We could grab a crate by two fingers of the right hand and swing them out onto the rack. It was hard, steady, physical work, but easy for an eighteen-year-old football player in the physical prime of his life. I don't remember how long we worked, but it was probably three or four hours from 5:00 to 9:00 P.M. We worked until the job was done and all the trucks were empty and ready for reloading in another part of the factory. It was a good job and made good money for part-time work for a college student. It was a good thing I had a strong back as well as a passable mind. Our PE credo was, "a strong mind in a strong body."

Despite Pearl Harbor and the impending war, my freshman year was idyllic. Aside from adjusting to the rigors of a college education, it was a time of delight getting away from home and out on my own. Every week or so there was a Wednesday night mixer in the Student Union area. These were dances with records played on a phonograph. It was a chance to mix and meet girls in a neat social setting. We played freshman football and then were able to go to all of the varsity games. We played San Diego State down in San Diego and the college hired a private train to take us down to the game and back the same night. There were records playing all the way so we could dance in a car without seats. I made friends for the most part with athletes and PE majors, but I also met many girls and had a couple of casual girlfriends during the year, but no serious relationships. The fraternity experience was interesting as I learned about that life and got to know my brothers really well by living with them. All in all it was a wonderful year of growth and excitement for me as we prepared for the war.

Chapter 24

Oxy—End of Freshman Year—LAS VEGAS

As the freshman year drew to a close, those of us who were working our way through college began to think about a summer job to earn enough money to come back to college in the fall. This was the spring of 1942, just after Pearl Harbor Day on December 7, 1941, and we were now at war with Germany and Japan. New defense plants were springing up all over the country so work was easy to come by. Several of us had heard of a magnesium plant being built near Las Vegas in a suburb now called Henderson. We decided to go up there to find work for the summer.

Conrad "Connie" Gullixson was not a particularly close friend of mine, but somehow we got paired up in our plans. Connie was a tall, string bean of a basketball player, while I was a short, stocky football player. We were not even in the same fraternity, but we had in common the fact that we were both Oxy freshmen who needed a job for the summer. Incidentally, Connie became a highly successful, influential, and rich attorney in a big law firm in the Bay Area. Connie has now passed away.

I had a 1931 Ford Model A coupe and Connie had a 1932 or '34 Chevy sedan. We decided to drive his car to Las Vegas the day after school was out. It was a long, long drive across the desolate desert on the narrow, two-lane highway from LA to Vegas in those days. There wasn't much in between and Barstow was only a gas station stop.

Upon arriving in Las Vegas, the first thing we did was to stop at the laborer's union hall and join the union. Neither Connie nor I had any particular skills as a carpenter or plumber, etc., and it took no skills to join the laborer's union, just a strong back and enough money to pay the union dues. We came to earn money, not to spend money, so the next thing was to find a place to stay temporarily. We found the Las Vegas High School, which had a nice green lawn out in front. We spent the first several nights sleeping on that lawn. The cops came by several times at night and shone their spotlights on us, but they didn't hassle us, since hobos sleeping out in the open was commonplace in those days.

Sleeping bags had only been patented in 1935 and weren't really available like they are today. When you speak of your sleeping roll, you meant a couple of blankets rolled up in a piece of canvas or tarp. You used your shoes or rolled up pants for a pillow. I think real sleeping bags were probably invented for WWII and then became a popular surplus item after the war. I know the first sleeping bag I owned was a GI surplus down bag I got for probably $10 at a surplus store after the war.

The next morning we were up early and in the union hall looking for an assignment. After a short wait, we were called up and given an address in downtown Las Vegas. We worked all day on a small construction job along with two or three black fellows that had shown up. At the end of the day, we told the boss we wanted to draw that day's pay and then quit. They really encouraged us to come back the next day because we were good workers and they wanted us back, but we said no, went to their office and drew our one-day paycheck.

We wanted to get on the big government magnesium project as housing was provided on that job and we had no place to live otherwise, so the next day we were back in the union hiring hall, after spending another night on the school lawn.

Sure enough, this time we were assigned to the plant in Henderson. This was about fifteen miles south of Vegas on the way to Boulder City where they had built Hoover Dam a few years before. There wasn't much between Vegas and Henderson at that time. It was mostly open desert with a couple of gas stations and bars along the way. The highway at that time was a two-lane paved road. Today it is a big freeway. On one side of the road was a tent city for the 5,000 men who worked building the plant from the ground up out in the open desert. The tents were like GI tents you have seen in the movies. There were six or eight men to a tent. They had wooden floors and netting all the way around. There was no air conditioning. Showers were in a special building down the road and there was a large mess hall. We walked to work across the two-lane highway to the construction site on the other side.

We started out our first day with a pick and shovel digging a hole in the desert for a basement or foundation for a large building. We looked like a picture of a chain gang in the movies or like a bunch of ants crawling all over this hole in the ground, moving a shovel full of dirt from the bottom of the hole step-by-step to a higher level and finally out on the top. It was June and the temperature was about 104 degrees and there was no shade. I survived and put in a full day. Connie was a skinny basketball player at about 6'

2" and 150 or 160 pounds. He was a good worker, but started drinking lots of water and pretty soon he got stomach cramps and had to knock off at about noon. He was able to walk around the plant site and, being a smart fellow, he looked around at other jobs better than what we were doing in that hole. I guess the hole in the ground was like boot camp in the Marine Corps. If you survived, you could go on to bigger and better things. As I remember, the pay scale was about the same for all laborer jobs, but some jobs were better than others. Connie talked to a foreman of the sheet metal crew working on the side of a building. The laborers' job was to set up the scaffolding and haul 4' to 8' metal sheets up to the journeymen who installed them. Connie arranged to get transferred to this crew and told me about the change that night back at our tent. I think I worked several days in the hole, but by the end of the week I also got a transfer to the sheet metal crew. It was a much better job, less tiring, cooler, and cleaner.

Of course, foremen were always looking for better-than-average workers, and I'm sure they talked between themselves about the good men they had and also those they would just as soon get rid of.

One day a foreman came over to me on the sheet metal crew and said, "Do you mind getting dirty?" I said, "No." He said he had a pretty good job inside a building in the shade and he needed a good man. He asked if I would be interested. I said, "Sure," so he took me over to a building where they were putting five one-hundred-pound blocks of carbon together to make huge anodes that would go into big vats where they would electrically separate the magnesium from the ore. The operation of the plant came later after I had left to go back to school. I spent the rest of the summer at that job and enjoyed it. We had a good crew and it was relatively easy work. We did get dirty from the carbon, but left our dirty clothes there and changed when we came to work in the morning and then took a shower and changed into clean clothes before going back to our tent each night.

The housing on the job was government subsidized. We made $80 a week, which was real good money in those days, and we only paid $10 a week for room and board for seven days of the week. I probably spent less than $5 a week for fun, entertainment, and incidentals, so I was able to save at least $65 a week toward my next year of college. By working ten weeks up there from mid-June through July and August I was able to save $650. Oxy is an expensive school, like Harvard and Stanford, but a year's tuition was only $400 a year then. I could have gone to UCLA for about $50 in 1942, but I didn't have the high school grades to get into that school. I don't believe the California State University system had been started yet at that time, so my only other choice would have been a junior college.

There were 5,000 men (no women) living in our tent city in the middle of the desert. It was the third largest town or encampment in Nevada at that time. Only Las Vegas and Reno were bigger than that tent city. I don't think Boulder City had 5,000 residents at that time.

One of our tent-mates was a Mormon from Utah. I remember he wore a set of long johns, which he never took off. It was a part of their religion and they were blessed or something. They had three little holes in them on the chest that had some special significance. We got along fine and I guess this experience of living in close quarters with strangers was an important part of growing up and learning tolerance for your fellow man and people who are different from you.

I was very strong for my age and size and I always liked to roughhouse, although I was never mean-spirited about grappling with others. I remember, one time, picking up the Mormon and throwing him across the tent. He landed on his bed or cot and busted it all up. I helped him take the pieces down to the commissary to turn it in for a new bed. No questions were asked.

Another time, I threw a fraternity brother across the living room in the frat house. He landed on a chair, breaking the arm off it. He and I were responsible for getting that chair repaired. One time five or six of us were rough housing on the stairwell in the house when I threw a fraternity brother, my best friend, down the stairs where he hit the banister and broke a couple of ribs. We had to take him to the college infirmary to get him taped up.

We were into WWII and the draft was on . Every boy (man) in America had to register for the draft when he was eighteen or before he turned nineteen. My birthday is in September, so I had to register before then. I registered in Las Vegas, Nevada. I'll never forget that momentous day, or where I was that summer of 1942.

There were about five or six Oxy guys working in Henderson that summer and we would get together once in a while to have some fun. On Saturday or Sunday we decided to go down to Lake Meade for a swim. We had our sack lunch from the commissary so we stopped and got a quart or half-gallon of milk each to drink with lunch. We didn't have any ice chests in those days, so when we got to the lake we put the milk in the water and weighted the cartons down with rocks. We took a swim and horseplayed in the water for awhile. I didn't hurt anyone that day. When we ate our lunch and got into our milk, we discovered that it had all turned sour in the 104-degree heat. It was a total waste.

We left the job about the end of August to go back to school. Connie and his family had visited in the High Sierra and he had been trout fishing, so we decided to take a little two- or three-day vacation in the high country before school started. We drove to Kings Canyon National Park and camped out for a few days. Connie introduced me to trout fishing and we caught quite a few, which we ate. I thought it was the most magnificent country I had ever seen. I have spent the rest of my life hiking, camping, and exploring many parts of our grand mountain chain and I give Connie full credit for introducing me to the wonderful Sierra Nevada and trout fishing. It was a great and deserving vacation after a hard summer of work in the heat of the desert.

Chapter 25

Let's Go Pro

From the eleventh grade on I was a first string starter on every football team I played on—eleventh grade: tackle, twelfth grade: guard, college freshman: end, sophomore: blocking back and linebacker.

Occidental College is a small Ivy League-type college in Los Angeles. Oxy plays football with schools like Cal Tech, Pomona, Whittier, and Redlands. It was average for a small school and won its share of games.

I started Oxy in the fall of 1941, just before Pearl Harbor. My high school football coach, Meb Schroeder, helped me get a partial football scholarship there. Otherwise, I worked my way through college paying my own way. I played two years in my freshman and sophomore years.

Oxy had decided to go a little more big-time in football in 1940 and hired "Gloomy Gus" Henderson as head coach. Gus had been the USC coach from 1919 to 1924 and was the first coach to make USC big time, winning many games. He coached the Detroit Lions in the NFL in 1939. A sportswriter gave him the name "Gloomy Gus" because at USC he would play his team down all week in practice and then come out and smash opponents on Saturday. The appellation "Gloomy Gus" stuck with him for the rest of his life. Gus scheduled bigger, tougher teams for

Oxy, like Fresno State, San Jose State, and Loyola.

I didn't want to be drafted into the Army, so I enlisted in the Marine Corps and was called to active duty on July 1, 1943. I was sent right back to Oxy in the V-12 program, which was an officers candidate program, because I had two years of college education.

In my sophomore year I played for Gloomy Gus as a blocking back and a linebacker. Our assistant coach and line coach was Pete Mehringer, an Olympic Gold Medal wrestler from Kansas whose nickname was the "Kansas Whirlwind." In 1932 as a Kansas University sophomore, he won the Gold Medal in the Los Angeles Olympics, being the first time a Kansas University athlete ever won the gold. After the Olympics he returned to KU to play football and was a 214-pound All American offensive tackle. He went on to a professional football career with the Chicago Cardinals and became a professional wrestler in the early days of television. Pete is in the National Wrestling Hall of Fame Distinguished Member, class of 1983.

In 1943 Oxy had about 1,000 Navy and Marine cadets on campus and would have had the greatest football team in its history with all of those able-bodied men, but Oxy, in all its wisdom decided to cancel football until the end of the war.

I was in the prime of my life and playing football was very important to me. What to do? Coach Mehringer's pro team worked out at Griffith Park in the evenings. These were the best players from all over the country who were living in Los Angeles at the time. There were players from USC and UCLA, Notre Dame, Ohio State, etc. They weren't paid $8 million a year in those days. Most men had a day job, but they were the best football players around.

There were no NFL teams in the West at that time, no Rams, Chargers, or 49ers. Men who wanted to play professional football played in the Pacific Coast League.

As I was itching to play more football, I went down to the park one evening and saw Pete. I asked him how you could get on the team. He said come on down and try out, so I did. After several hard evening practices, we had a team scrimmage on a Saturday to see who would make the team.

Well, I became the first-string guard with all-American Pete at the other guard. As I was in the Marine Corps, I played under an assumed name, Joe Knox from Tennessee.

Here is how I worked it. I would line up for roll call and muster at 5:00 P.M. on the Oxy quad as a Marine. Then I would break ranks and go over to my mother's house where I had my car parked, a Model A Ford. My mother and sister lived just across the street from campus—my sister started Oxy that year. Marines were not supposed to have cars, so mine was secretly parked at her house. Then I would drive to the field and practice football three hours at night and play games every Sunday. After practice, I would come home and my mother would feed me dinner, then I would walk back to campus.

I was only nineteen years old with only two years' of college experience, playing pro football with mostly twenty-two- to thirty-year-old men who had been stars at all the big schools in the country, and I was from little old Oxy. Pete was then thirty-three years old and as good as anyone on the field.

Of course, I was in the best shape of my life. The Marines got me up at 6:00 A.M. for a half hour or so of calisthenics. We had close order drill with rifles during the day, and as I was still a PE major, I had some activity or calisthenics classes during the day, and then I would practice football for three hours in the evening.

I never had any injuries that year even though we played all the big boys from San Diego, San Francisco, and Los Angeles (two teams). As I was being paid $21 a month in the Marine Corps—the extra money from football made me a pretty rich man (kid) for those days. Besides, it was fun.

After the fall season of playing professional football while I was in the Marine Corps, I went about my business of winning WWII by spending two years in the Pacific. When I returned home from the war in 1946 I enrolled as a student again at Oxy. I was mustered out of the service and went directly to summer school.

When the fall season arrived, I went over to Griffith Park and found the pro footballers were still practicing there, so I tried out for the team and was hired on as a first-string guard for the Los Angeles Mustangs. I played there for two more years while I was an undergraduate student at Oxy.

Since it was my practice to always be on the lookout for work, I was fortunate to be hired by Oxy as the junior varsity football coach in 1946, and the freshman coach in 1947 while still a student and physical education major. Our JV team was undefeated, untied, and unscored on. We scored sixty-nine points total during the season, our opponents zero. I had a great bunch of fellow students to work with that year; many of them were my fraternity brothers.

Late in the 1947 season I tore up my left knee badly and that was the end of my football playing career. There was no insurance program, nor was there the kind of medical care in those days such as we have today, so I've had a bum knee for the rest of my life. It is still swollen and sore today as I write this.

As an interesting side note, a human life was considered worth $20,000 in those days and each limb was worth $5,000, so for my left leg I was given a 25 percent permanent disability and a $5,000 payoff which helped toward buying our first home.

Chapter 26

Hawaii

Hawaii is one of the prime vacation spots of America. Probably most everyone in Oroville, California—where I now reside—has been there at one time or another. Our family has had a particular relationship to Hawaii for many years.

My uncle Ross was fire chief of Hickam Field on Pearl Harbor Day. The field was bombed and shot up and many planes were lost on the ground. One Japanese bullet was lodged in their bedstead in their house. Ross and his brother Jack were both retired Los Angeles City firemen and Jack became fire chief of Wheeler Field, near Schofield Barracks, where he remained all through the war and for many years thereafter.

I was in the Navy in WWII and was in the Philippines when the war was over and we were eventually directed to sail our station tanker home to San Francisco for decommissioning. Our great naval vessel could travel at ten knots (miles) per hour so it took us thirty days to sail home. We stopped by Pearl Harbor on our route home for some minor repairs so I was able to visit with my aunts and uncles at that time.

When I played professional football in the Pacific Coast League after the war, one of our opponents was the Hawaiian Warriors in Honolulu. Our team flew over and played a couple of games in Aloha Stadium, which afforded me another opportunity to visit my relatives who were still living there.

Then a few years later my mother and sister went over to the islands to work at Schofield. They lived with a lovely Filipino family, the Valderamas, in the town of Wahiawa located in the middle of the island. This gave us another nice connection to Hawaii. One of the Valderama girls was a symphony-class violin player who came to the mainland to perform. The Hawaiians don't speak of coming to the "States" but coming to the "mainland". After all, they now are one of our fifty states.

In the '60s I had the opportunity to fly to the islands again to do some missionary work on behalf of Optimist International. Hawaii was included in the Pacific Southwest District and had one or two clubs there. We wished to expand, so a small group of us went over to promote the growth of Optimism in that area. I was fortunate in being the first person in the group to recruit a new member into Optimism in the islands.

In 1967 our son Bob graduated from high school. He was a hotshot surfer in those days. Our daughter Deanna was graduating the following year and we promised her a family-style vacation as a present. A trip to Hawaii would cover both kids' graduation presents. Bev's mother had died shortly before this and her dad was at loose ends so he also joined us on this trip.

We made quite a sight at LAX as we prepared to load up for the Islands. Bev and I each had our own set of golf clubs and bags. We were planning to stay for nearly a month so we had luggage and equipment for five of us for that length of time and Bob was carrying his surfboard under his arm.

The plane did make the trip okay with all of us and all of our gear on board. We rented a car and an apartment in Kailua, over the Pali on the backside of Oahu from Honolulu. Bob went surfing on the day we landed and on the day we left and he rarely missed a day in between. We all had a wonderful time pursuing our own interests. Bev and I played golf nearly every day on many different courses. Deanna spent days tanning, soaking up the scenery, and watching Bob surf. We drove all over the island and showed Dad all of the natural beauty and "touristy" sights as well. We flew to visit the other islands and enjoyed their bounty as well. Nowadays many people fly direct to enjoy the outer islands and avoid the congestion of Honolulu, but remember, our trip was over forty years ago and things were different then.

From the above, you can see that our family has had many warm and friendly experiences and relationships with the kind and generous people of our fiftieth state: Hawaii. If you have never been there, it is time for you to go and visit one of the greatest vacation spots in the USA. If you have been there before, it may be time for another trip to try something new and different.

Anyone for football, surfing, golf, swimming, or sunbathing?

Chapter 27

Politics

Why does one grow up to be a Democrat or a Republican? Many people become one or the other just because of what their parents believe. Politics may not be discussed much in the home, but small, incidental comments over the period of growing up must have some accumulative effect. My family were Democrats. I don't know why. Aunt Julia and her mother were from Missouri and Uncle Jack was a native Californian. I'm sure Jack and Julia didn't discuss their party affiliation before they decided to get married.

The first election I remember was when Franklin Roosevelt first ran for president. I was about eight years old at the time and knew we were for Roosevelt. I remember Republican kids at school making disparaging remarks about Democrats being a bunch of drunks, as we were against prohibition and they were for it.

Uncle Jack took me to the Hollywood Bowl to hear FDR give a speech when he was a candidate. I don't remember what he said, but it was a significant, emotional experience for me and the first exciting event in my political life.

I don't know what attracted me to politics but I remember listening to conventions on the radio by myself even when the rest of the family was not interested. I'm glad that FDR ran enough times that I finally grew up and was able to vote for him the third time he ran.

Charles Lindberg was pro-Nazi before the war and he spoke one time in the Hollywood Bowl where I attended his speech. The place was packed and many people were giving him Hitler's raised arm salute and chanting "Heil Lindberg." I was a minority in the crowd that night but it was another highly emotional experience for me to see the passion of his supporters. I think I attended because he was an air hero and someone I wanted to see in person. This was about 1939 when I was around sixteen years old.

When I went to Oxy, I became friends with the son of Melvin Douglas, the movie star, and his wife Helen Gahagen Douglas, who was a congresswoman from Hollywood. I went to a party at their home in Beverly Hills one night and sitting on the piano was an autographed photo of FDR, my hero. Of course every Democrat congressperson in the country could have an autographed photo of FDR in their living room, but as an impressionable student of seventeen or eighteen I was highly affected.

I came from a middle-class background, but from the time of my parents' divorce when I was five, I recognized myself as an underdog and I have been for the underdog ever since, and a liberal democrat.

Aside from growing up in a Democratic family, I don't know what other factors had an influence on my political leanings, but the older I got, the more liberal I became.

A major benefit of going to college is to participate in bull sessions with people of all persuasions. You hear many points of view and it helps you refine your thoughts so you can express them more cogently. It is fun to debate with people of opposing views, but it also draws you closer to people who have similar views. I somehow developed a number of very close friends who were extremely liberal during the war years from 1941 to 1947. We were patriots who were willing to go to war and lay our lives on the line against Hitler and the axis and we were pro our allies, the Russians. We were not Communists, but we were sympathetic to their system and their great fight on the Eastern Front in Europe.

After the war I returned to Oxy and got back into active political events. I was never a Communist or associated with known party members other than my one fraternity brother, but I may have had some contact unknowingly . I remember going to a Young Communist League meeting at a big hall in Hollywood. Some woman was retiring from the YCL and admitted that night that she had really been a Communist for many years.

As many movies relate, there is *the* liberal professor on every college campus. We had one at Oxy. She was an outstanding teacher in the biology department and trained many future doctors. I was her lab assistant one semester and took several classes from her. We became good friends and discovered our mutual interest in liberal causes. We started a small group called Students for Federal World Government (SFFWG). This may have been a Communist front organization, but if it was I was never aware of it. On a couple of my professional football trips to Hawaii I combined the football with political activity by giving speeches in favor of SFFWG at the University of Hawaii.

There are still people violently opposed to the United Nations and want the US out of it, whereas SFFWG was a step beyond the UN, League of Nations, or NATO in world organizations. It is fun to be active when you are young. Students for Federal World Government is long gone and I don't think we did any harm to anyone by espousing our beliefs.

As I have moved through my life I have become more upwardly mobile and most of my friends, neighbors, and business associates have increasingly become conservative Republicans. Although I got off of my soapbox long ago, I am known in most of my social organizations as their "token" Democrat.

One of my children is a very conservative right-winger and my wife is a registered Republican, but I think she votes about the way I think as I research the propositions and candidates for both of us. When she goes into that polling place she puts her own mark down. I don't know what it is and that's the way it should be.

Nixon's first run at politics was for congressman against Helen Gahagen Douglas, the incumbent. He started and ended his political career with dirty tricks. He called Helen a Communist and won the election. Of course, I hated him the rest of his life. I did shake hands with Nixon at an Optimist Convention one time on the stage when he was our speaker. I saw President Eisenhower at Disneyland one time when he was our president. Estes Kefauver was a senator from Tennessee and a fraternity brother who ran for president, but he did not receive the Democratic nomination. He and Bob Dole, another candidate, were both Kappa Sigmas and fraternity brothers of mine. Another Kappa Sigma was governor of Texas and I met and shook hands with him at a national fraternity convention. Harold Ickes was a famous secretary of the Interior in the Roosevelt administration and I believe his son was deputy White

House chief of staff for President Bill Clinton. Ickes' brother lived across the street from friends of ours in Coeur d'Alene, Idaho, and we enjoyed chatting about politics, FDR, and his brother Harold when we visited up there for several summers.

Of course, I always admired Jimmy Carter and voted for him every time I could as he is the first Carter we have ever had in the White House. I thought he did a pretty good job, but he won't be in the history books as one of our "best" presidents. However, I don't think there is much question that he will be regarded as one of our very best "ex-presidents" with all the good work that he has done. I never admitted being related to Billy Carter, but I sure claim Jimmy as a cousin, and maybe we are.

These are a few of the political experiences I have had as I have traveled through this life. They have been interesting and they have made politics interesting for me.

I never ran for elected public office until I was in my seventies. I finally ran for a recreation district board of directors and I was the top vote getter in two elections.

I'm glad to have been able to serve the citizens of my community by being elected at that late date.

Chapter 28

There are some events in a lifetime that are so momentous that most people remember where they were when something really big happened. The two most memorable times in my life were when President Kennedy was shot and Pearl Harbor Day.

I was a freshman in college and eighteen years old on that infamous Pearl Harbor day in 1941. I was still living at home and had a 1931 Model A Ford coupe which I drove back and forth to school. I was out in the backyard washing my car and had the radio on playing music, just like kids do today. It was around ten o'clock in the morning when the program was interrupted with the news flash. I was the first person in our family or neighborhood to know about the attack and I ran into the house to tell everyone about it. I will never forget that day or what I was doing.

The following summer I went to Las Vegas to work in a magnesium defense plant to earn money to go to college as a sophomore. I first signed up for the draft in Las Vegas as an eighteen year old. I guess they were after me , so sometime in 1942 I enlisted in the Marine Corps to avoid the draft. As I was a college student, I was able to get in the V-12 program which was an officers candidate program.

On July 1, 1943, they called me up, put me in a Marine uniform as a private, and sent me right back to Occidental College in the V-12 program. There was also a program where they would put you through medical school to become a doctor. I had been a PE major, but I changed to a pre-med major and entered that program. I took a full load of college pre-med courses plus close order drill (marching), and special calisthenics, courtesy of the Marine Corps.

We didn't normally use rifles, but there was a big parade through downtown Los Angeles on Armistice Day, November 11, so they got us a bunch of rifles and we practiced with them for a couple of weeks and marched behind a 125-piece Marine band from San Diego. We were in olive uniforms but the band was in Marine dress blues and it was a thrill to be behind them. I guess we marched okay.

Our leader was a captain who had been in the fighting on Guadalcanal and we were proud of him too. At the beginning of the war about all we had in the Pacific were Marines, but as the Army became bigger, they decided they needed more Navy ensigns to run the landing boats up on the beach, than Marine second lieutenants to lead Marine platoons. So they asked for volunteers to transfer from the Marines to the Navy. The biggest incentive was that we would get out in the Pacific to fight the Japs sooner. After another year and a half of college classes under the Marines, many of us were anxious to get into the war and get out there to the fighting. Another factor for me personally was the fact that they dropped the medical program, so I didn't have a chance to become a medical doctor after all.

Several hundred of us volunteered to transfer so they sent us by troop train across the country to Asbury Park, New Jersey, to a hotel where they had the pre-midshipman school. We Marines were pretty tough and we had been poking fun at the Navy for

Midshipman Vernon Carter, USNR, Cornell University, Ithaca, New York, 1944

over a year now. There were many mixed emotions and sad faces the day we took off our Marine uniforms and put on "swab jockey," apprentice seaman uniforms with the white sailor hats.

After about six weeks at Asbury Park, which was just a holding situation, many of us were sent to Cornell University to a regular midshipman school where we were ninety-day wonders and became officers and gentlemen. We had classes in seamanship, gunnery, navigation, naval customs and lore, etc. Everything they taught in four years at the Naval Academy, they taught us in three months for the war.

After graduation as an ensign, I had a couple of weeks leave to see my family in California and then headed to San Francisco to wait to ship out. It seems we waited about a month. We were stationed in a BOQ (Bachelor Officer's Quarters) in a down-

Vernon Carter, Ensign, USNR, 1944–1946.

town hotel named the Bellevue. During that month I became engaged to an old high school girlfriend who was a student at Mills College in Oakland. After a few months she sent me a Dear John letter, so nothing came of that.

I was assigned to a station tanker in Eniwetok and traveled out there on a merchant ship. Four officers shared a cabin and the shower was full of cases of cigarettes. The sweet tobacco aroma was horrible. I had never spent much time aboard any kind of boat or ship, so I was seasick before we went under the Golden Gate Bridge and was sick for eighteen days until we got to Eniwetok. I couldn't stand it in the smelly cabin, so I set up a cot on the deck and slept out in the open, which was a little better.

Arriving at Eniwetok and joining my ship, I was west of Pearl Harbor for two years without any leave or a change of duty. I served on two similar ships, the USS *Whippet* and the USS *Gemsbok*. We were called station tankers and just swung on the anchor. Merchant tankers brought black fuel oil to us and then we gave it to aircraft carriers, battleships, cruisers and destroyers. We were a floating gas station. The smaller ships came alongside of us , but we got underway and went alongside the big aircraft carriers and battleships.

I did every job aboard ship except being captain, executive officer, or engineering officer. I was a lieutenant JG by the time the war was over. From the Marshall Islands we went to the Mariana Islands and eventually to the Philippines, where we liberated them. We were always behind the front and I was never involved in any fighting or ever fired a shot at the enemy.

My duty was much like the movie *Mr. Roberts,*

starring Jack Lemmon, Henry Fonda, and James Cagney. We moved from tedium to monotony but it was a job that had to be done. We celebrated VE Day in Eniwetok and VJ Day in Manila Harbor.

After the war was over, we were directed to come home to San Francisco. Our ship, which was a converted Liberty ship, could only go ten knots an hour so it took us thirty days of steady sailing across the pacific. We stood four-on and eight-off shifts for all thirty days. This means you stood a four-hour shift on duty around the clock, day and night. Then you ate and slept on your eight off, but you had to do all of your regular duties during that time too.

I did my duty as called upon but I wasn't particularly enamored with the military. We were offered the opportunity to stay in the reserve, but I was glad to be out and be finished with the military.

I did take full advantage of the GI Bill for education and completed my BA in PE, got an MS in education, and eventually got an Ed.D. in education. I never did get to be a medical doctor, although I think I could have been one if I had the chance.

We were just citizen soldiers who were willing to sacrifice our lives, if needed, to protect and save this wonderful country of ours. I was glad to do my small part, but I was glad when it was over so I could come home, get married and raise a family.

Chapter 29

Liberty Ships

The Japanese attack on Pearl Harbor on December 7, 1941, nearly wiped out the entire US Navy and left the United States in a very weakened position. We had begun to mobilize and rearm by supplying Great Britain with arms through the Lend-Lease Act two years after Hitler's attack on Poland in 1939, but we were far from ready for a war of our own.

The program that really won the war for us was our magnificent war production line. It was the fantastic number of planes, tanks, ships and armaments that our workforce, along with the help of "Rosie the Riveter," was able to produce in a very short time. It was that assembly line, as well as our valiant fighting men that won the war for us and our allies. We built thousands of airplanes and ships.

In addition to the aircraft carriers and battleships needed to replace those lost at Pearl Harbor, cargo ships were needed to carry our supplies throughout the world across both the Atlantic and the Pacific oceans.

The Liberty ships were one small but integral part of that armada. More than 3,000 identical ships were built from the same set of plans. A ship was constructed in only 56 days by newly-trained shipworkers, many of them women who had never before worked in construction.

I served on two Liberty ships, the USS *Whippet* and the USS *Gemsbok*. These were regular Liberty ships that had been converted to tankers. The outside steel hull, about one-half inch thick, was the only thing between 5,000 tons of oil and the sea outside. I was cargo officer of the ship, responsible for loading and dispensing our black oil. A Liberty ship was a 10,000-ton ship about 100 feet long and ours had a crew of about 100 men. I spent two years of my life aboard these ships.

Many of the ships were mothballed to the Reserve Fleet in Suisun Bay near San Francisco, where they were scrapped for metal years after the war. Much of that steel was shipped back to Japan as scrap steel for their manufacturing plants.

There is one sole survivor of the Liberty ships that stormed Normandy beachheads on D-day. It is the SS *Jeremiah O'Brien* which is stationed in San Francisco today in 2008. She was launched in 1943 to carry supplies to our allies in war-torn Europe. The *O'Brien* participated in the Normandy landings. She safely crossed the English Channel eleven times, landing at Utah and Omaha beaches, and was part of what President Franklin D. Roosevelt then referred to as the "bridge of ships."

After the war the *O'Brien* was mothballed in Suisun Bay. She lay there for thirty-three years awaiting the scrappers. She was not, however, to meet the same fate as her sister ships. In 1979 a group of Merchant Marine veterans decided to preserve her as a living memorial to the men and women who served, manufactured, and perished aboard Liberty ships. The *O'Brien* became the first restored, live and steaming ship museum in the country.

Each year the *O'Brien* makes a cruise from San

Francisco to Sacramento and back. It is a nine-hour trip one way. In 2004 I purchased a one-way passage for $175 for a trip to San Francisco. So, after fifty-eight years, I was able to stand on the bridge of a WWII Liberty ship while she was under way. I must admit it brought tears to my eyes, and as I write this in 2008, it still brings tears to my eyes. I must admit to being a sentimentalist.

Chapter 30

I spent nine months of my life on Eniwetok atoll in the Marshall Islands in the South Pacific. We speak of many of these islands as "South Pacific" but the Marshalls are really ten degrees north of the equator. That travel journey was courtesy of Uncle Sam during WWII. I was on a station tanker doing a dull but very important job for two years in the Pacific. We were an anchored gas station and the gas was not $2.00 a gallon either. Merchant tankers brought oil to us and then we in turn fueled aircraft carriers, battleships, cruisers, and destroyers to go out and fight.

Eniwetok had been held by the Japanese so we blasted it with big guns before we went ashore and had knocked down every single tree and bush on the island. When I arrived it was a pile of sand and coral about ten feet above sea level and the only thing of value or interest there was the officers' club where you could get all the beer you wanted to drink or could go swimming in the lagoon.

From there we went to Ulithi in the Caroline Islands on the way into Leyte Gulf and the liberation of the Philippines. I spent a year there where I had a chance to explore the islands of Leyte, Samar, and Luzon—eventually getting into Manila Harbor.

This vast expanse of islands across the southwest Pacific is becoming a favorite tourist destination nowadays. They are colorful and quaint as well as being of historical and nostalgic value to the veterans of WWII. Hotels and tourist amenities are being built on many of the small and out-of-the-way places and are easily reached by air today. I have heard from friends that Papua, New Guinea, is particularly interesting and a good tourist stop.

In addition to my unasked-for opportunities during the war I have spent considerable time in the far corners of our globe. Bev and I have had a lovely trip through Australia and New Zealand. It is a good adventure across the world from us that one of any age can enjoy. Most good trips include stop-overs in Fiji and Tahiti on the way to and from so one can get a look at some of these great island communities on the way.

We have also been to Japan, China, Hong Kong, Beijing, Shanghai, and Macao on the Asian Continent.

A couple of years ago I went to Indonesia on a Global Volunteers trip to teach English to the Indonesians for a couple of weeks. We visited the island and beaches of Bali and were stationed in the city of Yogyakarta on Java. It was a most exciting trip as we worked with preschoolers to adults to help them with their English and also had an opportunity to see the sights and get to know the people well as we lived with them.

Indonesia is the third most populous country in the world after China and India and is the most populous Moslem country in the world. Although they have had a dictatorship regime ever since their independence from the Netherlands after WWII, the Indonesian people are very gentle, kind, and friendly, and I enjoyed very much getting to know them.

In fact all of the people of the Western islands that I have had the pleasure to meet and deal with have been most cordial, friendly, and laid back. We have had many fun experiences with them. Late one night when we were hitchhiking back to our hotel in Tahiti a group in a pickup truck stopped, put us in the back of the truck, and took us all the way to our hotel which was some distance out of Papeete.

One charming young schoolteacher friend on Java called me "Grandfather" whenever she addressed me in deference and respect to my advanced age.

If you would like to put a little more adventure into your travel plans, "think South Pacific."

Chapter 31

Home from the War

During WWII, I was on a ship west of Pearl Harbor for two years. We did get into Manila on the Philippines during its liberation, but that's the only time we had even seen a woman for two years. We did stop at Pearl Harbor on our way home and I was able to contact my mother telling her that I would be along home pretty soon.

My mother and sister lived within a block of Occidental College where my sister and I had gone to school. My sister was in a sorority and had a particularly good friend named Beverly, who was also a good friend of my mother.

The big Pan Hellenic all-sorority dance was coming up about the time I was due home. Beverly had just broken up with a sailor so had no date for this big dance.

Shirley said, "You don't want to miss the big dance. If my brother gets home in time, you can take him to the dance."

Bev said, "Oh, I don't know. I don't care if I don't go to the dance. Your brother won't know anyone there and it will just be a blind date."

Shirley said, "Well, he's a pretty good guy and it will be nice for him on his first days home."

Bev said, "I'll think about it. We'll see if he gets here in time."

We steamed under the Golden Gate Bridge in the

middle of the week. Boy was that a sight for sore eyes! My battle station was on the bow on the ship and I was the first person on our ship under the bridge. It was sort of like the kids in the movie *Titanic.*

We anchored in San Francisco Bay and the men who lived on the West Coast were granted a weekend pass right away as we had been away so long. I arranged a flight into LA on Friday and was greeted by my folks. I was in my gray work uniform—as you could travel in one at that time—and only had a ditty bag with me.

At the first opportunity, Shirley said, "The big Pan Hellenic dance is tomorrow night at the Beverly Hills Hotel. Would you like to go with a friend of mine named Beverly?" That sounded okay to me so I said, "Sure!"

It was a formal dance and I didn't have a set of blues with me so I went down to fraternity row to do some scrounging. I found a buddy I had played football with before the war. He had gotten home before me and was back in school. He wasn't even in my fraternity, but he willingly loaned me his blues and the fit was pretty good as we were about the same size.

I didn't have a car, so Beverly came over and picked me up in her 1934 Chevy. That's the first time I had ever seen her or met her. She was a nice-looking blond and we set out for Beverly Hills, just the two of us. She still had trepidation, as she didn't think I would know a soul there. As it happened, lots of Oxy guys had gotten back from the war by then and I knew a whole bunch of people, maybe more than she knew. We danced well together and had a really good time.

I flew back to Frisco Sunday evening. A few weeks later, after we had put our ship in mothballs up in Suisun Strait, I came home to get mustered out of the service. I was to go to Chavez Ravine near Griffith Park, where they later built Dodger Stadium. There was no public transportation to that naval reserve station as it was very isolated up in the hills above LA. Shirley said, "Call Bev, she will loan you her car." I did, and got mustered out of the Navy with her car. When I returned it, I asked her for a date and that went pretty well, so about a year later we got married! It was a good blind date. We've been married sixty-two years this year, 2009.

Chapter 32

Beverly Jean Gillett Carter

A positive aspect in my life started when I met Bev on my return home from the service. Beverly Jean Gillett was born in Eau Claire, Wisconsin. Her mother was Grace Eleanor Thompson Gillett and her father was Alden Cherry Gillett. Bev had one brother, Fred, who was two years older than she. Her mother was of Norwegian stock as her grandmother, Hilda Thompson, immigrated to the United States from Norway when she was a young child. She lived to be ninety-four years old right here in America. Alden's family were somewhat well-to-do lumber people, and a small lumber mill town in Wisconsin is named Gillett, purportedly after them. Bev's parents were both college graduates and her mother was a schoolteacher.

The Gilletts lost most of their wealth in the Great Depression, so Alden's family moved to Pasadena, California, where Bev grew up. Bev was an outdoor, tomboy type and played touch football with the neighborhood kids. She was known as a "good pass catcher." She went to John Marshall Junior High School where she played the trumpet in the orchestra and was a drum majorette in the band. One of her activities there was to blow the trumpet as the flag was raised every day. She went two years to Pasadena Junior College before finishing her education at Occidental College in Los Angeles. She received an AA

Beverly Gillett, junior–zeta–coed. Occidental College, 1946.

degree from Pasadena Junior College with a secretarial and business background. She spent two years working at Arnold's Jewelry store before she started college.

Bev lived in a college dormitory, Haines Hall, at Occidental which, incidentally, is the same dorm that President Barack Obama lived in some forty years later. After she graduated, some fourteen girls who had also lived in this dorm started a round-robin letter that has been making the rounds now for over sixty years and is still going strong. This group has kept this relationship together all of these many years through reunions on cruise trips and other meetings. They have traveled all over the world together.

Bev met me in May of 1946. She started her senior year in September of that year when she moved to her sorority house from the dorm. We enjoyed a very activity-filled romance with "pinning" when I gave Bev my fraternity pin. Several months later we became engaged with all the traditional formality of the fraternity brothers gathering at the sorority house to serenade the newly engaged couple. At the same time this was announced to Bev's sorority with the "passing chocolates" ceremony where the date of the upcoming marriage was told with a poetic proclamation given to each sorority member along with a chocolate. Bev graduated in June 1947 with a BA in sociology and a minor in psychology.

After a summer-long honeymoon, Bev was able to procure a good job as executive secretary to the western region sales manager for the Coca-Cola Company. She kept that job until she became pregnant with our first child, Bobbie.

I was in college for one more semester after our marriage, and for that semester we lived in some veterans housing units on the campus.

Bev has been a helpmate all through our life together helping me in my many pursuits by typing all my documents and manuscripts. I couldn't have accomplished what I have without her help.

Chapter 33

Marriage

How do you encapsulate sixty years of marriage into a few hundred words? The best you could do would be to hit a few highlights. It would be more like an essay on marriage, rather than a story or vignette.

I think the birth of the first child of a union is special. Perhaps because our first little guy had the nine-month colic, that is what made him so special. We practically lived with his grandparents, as someone had to hold him about twenty hours a day to keep him from crying.

I was going to summer school at USC when our second child Deanna was born sixteen months later. Beverly woke me about 5:00 A.M. and said something was happening. I said, "You won't be able to wait until I get home from school?" which would be about 1:00 P.M. "If I'm not going to school I'll roll over and I can sleep in." Fifteen minutes later we were in the car heading for the hospital.

The biggest event at an early age in our lives was when I won a Fulbright Exchange Teacher scholarship in the Netherlands. We were babes in the woods and had never been abroad, but we packed up our two little kids, two and three years old, and took off for a year. During that time we visited nineteen countries in Europe and our two kids learned to speak fluent Dutch so that they could interpret for us by the end of the year.

A memoir like this can include some advice to the lovelorn as sixty years indicates that we have been successful, at least by sticking together that long.

Success means there must be give and take all along the way and certainly teamwork. We have always been a great team. Even today, when I am sawing wood with a chain saw, Beverly holds the wood on the sawhorse so I don't cut my foot off. We were fortunate that we both had common goals. This certainly helps. We were Depression babies and have the same ideas on spending and saving and we are both goal oriented so together we set goals to accomplish.

Our biggest argument is over who is going first, as we both feel that neither could live without the other. I guess an airplane crash is best so we can go together. I know that if I were alone, I would have to get married within a week, because all of my clothes would be dirty and I would be starving to death.

Chapter 34

Profound Moments

The birth of your first child is a profound moment in everyone's life. What an awe inspiring experience to see this new creature that you have been responsible for bringing into the world. It is the ultimate conclusion of love, marriage, union, and creation. It is the essence of God's wonderful plan for procreation.

Our first child was Bob. It's nice to have a boy first. He was okay, but suffered nine-month colic. It took two pairs of parents and grandparents to survive that first nine months of listening to him cry and caring for him and holding him.

When Deanna, was born sixteen months later, we were much more relaxed and laid back as parents. Bob was a happy, relaxed little guy by now and Deanna was a sweet happy baby and a delight to us.

None of our children were "planned" but were welcomed as the natural course of life. We sort of figured this was the end of our family. We had each reproduced ourselves and I was a firm believer in and a member of Zero Population Growth at the time.

We had a wonderful life. I was upwardly mobile in my teaching profession . We had spent a year in Europe, where our two children learned to speak fluent Dutch. They had visited eight or ten countries and for the first thirteen–fourteen years of their lives, they were two of the nicest, best-behaved children in the world. We always received compliments about them. Life was good.

Ten years after Deanna's birth, Bev became pregnant again. She was thirty-seven years old at the time. I was principal of a junior high school and although this event was a surprise, we were happy and looking forward to this new addition to the Carter clan. Bev was healthy and had a normal pregnancy, but none of her births were easy. I guess a lot of drugs were administered during delivery, but it was normal.

In the first few weeks we noticed that Carol was expelling milk through her nostrils while eating. Our pediatrician was an older man who was a personal friend and member of my Optimist Club. He explained that some babies have to learn to close the air gap to the nose while eating and she would get the hang of it soon. I think he knew there was something wrong at that time, but he didn't say anything to us.

In the next few weeks it seemed that Carol didn't respond to things quite like our other kids had. We began to take her to other doctors and get tests, etc. It turned out that she was profoundly retarded and had abnormal brain waves. The cause was unknown.

We kept her home with us for seven years. Bev fed her every mouthful of food she ate and gave her constant new-baby care for that time. Her brother and sister were great with her. We had a pool and she loved to go in the water and stretch out on her brother's surfboard in the pool.

Carol had never learned to walk, but her brother Bob had been working with her secretly in the bedroom and on Mother's Day, when she was four and a half years old, he brought her out and had her walk unaided over to her mother! That was a very special Mother's Day.

When she was seven, we made the decision to have her placed in Lanterman State Hospital. That was the toughest decision of our lives. The state of California has been taking care of her ever since and we are very grateful to the state for the wonderful care she has had. She has been in many institutions, hospitals, and care homes. She is presently in a six-person care home where she has her own bedroom and waterbed, and receives excellent care. Carol is now forty-nine years old and confined to a wheel chair. She is still a happy person but of course has a very limited life.

I hope she goes before we do so we can see her to the end of her sweet but special life.

Catalina

When I was a young teacher, I always had a summer job, to help us move ahead with the family income. One of my fraternity brothers came from Catalina Island and several of our brothers had various jobs over there during the summers even before we graduated. Paul Xanthos ran the recreation program for the city of Avalon. John Marincovich worked on the dock when the big white steamer came in at noon. I inquired of my buddies and they said that Avalon hired extra policemen for the summer when the crowds came on the big ship for the day. Our daughter Deanna was born on August 3, 1950, and my wife Bev and I went over to Catalina a couple of weeks later to look things over for the following summer. We walked all over the island, up and down the many hills, and I remember Bev started hemorrhaging quite badly as she wasn't healed up yet from the delivery.

I applied and was accepted for the next summer as a policeman for the city of Avalon. I wore a uniform, badge, and gun but didn't have much special training. Our little family of four arrived by boat just after school was out and we found an apartment at the Tree House Inn, which had cooking facilities and refrigerator shared with other residents.

The SS *Catalina* was known as the "Great White Steamer." She was built for one million dollars by

Catalina Island owner and chewing gum mogul William Wrigley in 1924. She plied the ocean between Wilmington and Avalon daily between 1924 and 1975. Along with a twenty-six-mile ocean voyage, a $2.25 round-trip ticket offered 2,200 passengers big-band orchestra music for dancing, children's entertainment by clowns and magicians, and adult amenities such as leather settees and drinks from a shipboard bar. She was known for her crisp white paint job and deep, melodious horn that announced her departures.

During WWII, the 1,766-ton vessel was used as a military transport. The cruise-like ship was designated a Los Angeles historical cultural landmark and a state historical landmark and placed on the National Register of Historical Places. She made 9,807 Catalina channel crossings and ferried twenty-five million people to Catalina.

I went to work at noon when the Great White Steamer arrived each day. My job was to keep the two thousand passengers moving away from the dock to prevent a traffic jam in the streets where the other tourists were always gathered to watch the arrival. I was the only police officer in Avalon on duty at that time of day and it was an intense job trying to be everywhere at once.

Then my job was to patrol along the beachfront for eight hours to keep the peace between the 2,000 visitors and residents. Beer drinking was not allowed on the beach at that time, so enforcing that restriction was also a big part of the job.

I bought a fourteen-foot dingy with a nine horse outboard motor so we were able to travel up and down along the coast snorkeling and diving. Both abalone and lobster were plentiful at that time and we lived off the sea all summer. We actually got tired of eating those two delicacies.

Bev and the kids spent the summer on the beach. Bob was two and a half and Dee had her first birthday on August 3. We lived about a block and a half from the beach and waterfront and they had a wonderful carefree summer. One evening as Bev was preparing dinner, she discovered that Bob was missing. He had wandered outside and had gone all the way back down to the beach and was playing in the water. I don't think he could swim yet at two and a half. Some kind soul rescued him and called the cops, but not me. I guess the other cop knew it was my kid so he walked him home as Bev came barreling down the block looking for him. The cop made a report of this so Bob made the police blotter for that escapade.

Another time Bob locked himself in the bathroom and Bev couldn't get him to open the door. Finally, in desperation, she called the police department. Another officer responded and climbed through the window and unlocked the door. Bob was once again on the police blotter.

It was illegal to have lobster traps around the island, but one night as a buddy, Bill Pearson, and I were snorkeling around in a little cove we spotted a metal trap below. The trap was about 4' x 3' x 3', made of heavy metal with a trap door in the middle and was quite heavy. It was down about twenty feet so my buddy took a dive for it. He didn't quite reach it so was coming back up when I dove for it. I went down and down and reached for the trap but was short, so I took another couple of strokes and caught the edge of the trap and started up. I was about out of breath and didn't think I would teach the top. I thought Bill would come back down and give me a hand but he just floated there like a jellyfish watching me. I was determined not to let go of the trap, so I kept groaning with every stroke and finally made it to the top where he did grab hold of the trap to help me get it to the rocks. It had seven lobsters in it, so after carefully putting them in our gunny sacks we tossed the illegal empty trap back in the water. They were um, um good.

The word got around that we were spending the summer at Catalina so everyone we knew came over to visit us that summer. We did have room to put up an extra couple or two and every single weekend of the summer we had houseguests, but it was fun and a great summer and vacation to remember.

Chapter 36

Fulbright Exchange Teacher

I have always been interested in geography, the world, and travel. I enjoyed geography in elementary school. It created a feeling of wonder and excitement for me. Perhaps it was part escapism from my early life of poverty. As I progressed in school I realized there was so much to learn, explore, and experience in this life and in our world, and I wanted to see as much of it as I could. I was always ready for a trip to go somewhere I had never been before. From my home on Benda Place, as a child before I

The Carter family at Christmas in Holland, 1952.

had a bicycle, I walked as far as my legs would carry me during a day, moving out in every direction from home exploring what to me was the unknown. I hiked a long way, clear to the other end of Hollywood to the famous HOLLYWOOD sign and climbed to the top of it. As a ten year old I climbed over the fence and explored the back lots and sets of Universal and Warner Brothers Studios. I would hide from the security cops as they made their rounds in their trucks. I hiked up and down the Los Angeles riverbed, once nearly cutting off a couple of toes on a broken bottle as I was walking bare footed.

When I was thirty years old I was a physical education teacher in a junior high school in Los Angeles. One day I looked on the bulletin board in the teachers lounge and saw an announcement about making applications for a Fulbright Exchange Teacher Scholarship in Europe. J. William Fulbright was an ex-teacher and professor who was a United States senator from Arkansas. Shortly after WWII Senator Fulbright came up with a wonderful idea. Most of the countries of the world owed the United States money after the war. Some of it would never be paid back and it was difficult for many countries to exchange their money for dollars and pay us back in dollars. Fulbright's idea was to allow countries to pay off some of these war debts in the local currency of their country for the peaceful and worthwhile project of exchanging students and teachers between their countries and the United States.

This sounded like a pretty good idea to me so I pulled an application blank off the wall, filled it out, and sent it in to Washington, D.C. Sometimes one makes his own fate and changes his entire life with certain decisions. In 1952 I was selected as the only man in the entire United States to go to Holland for a year to teach physical education to Dutch boys and girls.

At that time, Bev and I had two children: Bob, three, and Deanna, two years old. We packed some things, hopped into our old Chevy and drove from Los Angeles to New York where we sold the car. We sailed on the liner *Westerdam* to Rotterdam. From there we traveled by train to Paris, France where we purchased a used car, an Anglia, which is a British Ford. We drove this back to Holland and reported in at Haarlem, my assignment for the year.

I worked with two male physical education teachers in two schools and my workload for the week was four days, which gave me a three-day weekend every week. Bev and I had never been to Europe before and this is when our love for travel really took off. Some of the Fulbright scholars spent their extra money buying antiques, etc., and one even purchased a piano to bring back home. Bev and I, however, decided to spend all of our extra time and money trying to see everything we could.

We had both read a lot about the culture and history of Europe and we wanted to see as much as we could. Distances in Europe seem much shorter than in the United States. Holland is centrally located and we could drive from our home in Haarlem to Belgium, Luxembourg, or Germany in a couple of hours, which might be likened to driving from the California towns of Oroville to Stockton or maybe Fresno.

We succeeded in our quest. We put 20,000 miles on our Anglia in our years' stay there, which is a lot of miles for Europe in those days. We were in nineteen different countries; the only ones we missed were Finland and Portugal. We still have never been in those two countries.

We did visit all the major countries from Norway and England, to Yugoslavia in the east, and Spain in the west. Some of the more interesting and obscure places we visited included Trieste, Liechtenstein, Monaco, San Marino, Luxembourg, and the Vatican City.

After we got settled in Haarlem, Bev hired a nanny/mother's helper to help with the children and the necessary daily marketing. This was in the year 1952 and our apartment had no refrigerator. Her name was Riet Timmers, a nineteen-year-old girl whose father had a plumbing business and a mother who was a wonderful housewife. These folks did not have any grandchildren at that time. They adopted us as part of their family and we felt very comfortable with them. They had a vacation beach house on the North Sea and spent their summers there. The Timmers family invited our children to spend the summer with them on the beach. This gave Bev and me the opportunity to spend the summer traveling after the school year was over. With some trepidation, we agreed and took off. We went across central Europe through Germany, Austria, Switzerland, Italy, and Yugoslavia. We probably could have kept going on to Greece, Turkey, and Asia, but we really got homesick for the kids when we reached Yugoslavia, so we turned around and hightailed it back to Holland. We made it back across Europe in about three days. Were we ever glad to see those little kiddies! They had been having a perfect time at the beach all summer and had learned to speak fluent Dutch—so all of the people on the beach thought they were Dutch kids.

We were very fortunate to have that wonderful year in Europe. Travel-wise it was the highlight of our entire life and we consider Holland our adopted country. The Dutch people were so warm and kind to us and we still correspond with some of them after fifty years. We thank Senator Fulbright, also, for his inspirational idea of encouraging peace and friendship throughout the world.

The magnificent start in Europe when we were thirty years old got us started and we have been on the go ever since. We retired at age fifty-two and have spent the last thirty-three years traveling all over the world. I have been on every continent except Antarctica and have enjoyed a safari in Africa. Bev and I have been to China, Australia, New Zealand, Russia, and in '98 went to Peru and the Galapagos Islands.

We have gone alone many times, but have enjoyed traveling with our friends Joe and Ann Gray (Australia and New Zealand), brother Fred and his wife Lee (China, Panama Canal, Mediterranean, Galapagos), sister Shirley and her husband Bill (New England and eastern Canada), as well as many trips with the Oxy "round robins" and other groups of friends.

I still enjoy traveling very much. There is so much to see and so many places I have not seen yet.

A fun trip in 1999 was going back to Paris with two of my granddaughters Shanti and Kendra. I'm still looking forward to more travel.

Chapter 37

Our daughter, Deanna, was a very pretty blue-eyed, blond, baby and child. When we were in Holland in 1952–1953, we left our two children with our baby sitter, Riet, and her parents while we took a lengthy trip sightseeing in Europe. Their family had a beach house on the North Sea where they spent their summers. This was during our second summer there and Bob and Dee had learned to speak fluent Dutch by this time. In fact there were occasions when they were translating for us even though we had both picked up a smattering of Dutch ourselves. Riet's parents related to our children much as grandparents would and treated them lovingly in that manner, so we felt comfortable in leaving our two for such an extended trip as we had planned.

The kids played on the beach all summer and everyone around assumed they were Dutch children since they looked the part and were speaking in Dutch. Riet's parents did not speak any English so Dutch was the language they all used while together that summer.

One day a photographer happened along the beach taking snapshots and observing the children playing and having a good time. I'm sure he took many pictures of other children that day, but he also took a cute picture of our three-year-old Dee playing in the sand. He asked Riet, who was attentive near-

129

by if he could use or publish the picture. No money or contract exchanged hands, and I doubt that even a consent form was signed at that time in Holland in 1953. However, Deanna's picture soon appeared on the cover of the most popular women's magazine in Holland. The name of the magazine was , *Moeder en Kind*. This means Mother and Child and was similar in popularity to the *Womens Home Journal* in America.

When we came back from our summer trip, we found that the magazine had already been published and we have a copy that we have cherished and enjoyed all these years.

Neither Dee, Riet or we, her parents got any money for her to be a cover girl, nor did we get anything for suing the publishing company for using her picture without our permission, but it was an unusual and happy experience for our family. A copy of the cover of the magazine is shown on the next page.

Deanna Carter on cover of Moeder en Kind.

Chapter 38

Jobs

I have been earning money since I was five years old. I figured you could always get a job if you were of average or better intelligence, if you were willing, and if you had a positive attitude. I think I have always made a good impression on a job interview.

I hate mechanics and have no skills at anything but my chosen profession where I went to school and learned the various facets of education as I progressed in that vocation.

In education, I have been a teacher, coach, counselor, health coordinator, vice-principal, principal, registrar of students (college level), and superintendent of schools. I have taught every grade from seven through twelve and adult education. I have also taught square dancing and been a caller.

I was blessed with a strong back and a healthy body and most of my early jobs were of a menial-, physical-, or laboring-type without any specific skills. I have been a ditch digger and common laborer, starting at the very bottom of the wage scale. I was able to work my way up to sheet metal helper and mason tender by my willing attitude, strength, and work habits, which outshone other common laborers with less drive and motivation than I had.

I have also been a janitor, gardener, and truck driver, but I never learned to drive a semi. When I was young, I was a lifeguard at a Boy Scout camp all summer and as a little child, as previously described, was a magazine salesman.

When I became a teacher and had two small children, I always had many extra jobs to help support our growing family. My wife never worked an outside job for any appreciable amount of money, so I was the sole wage earner in our family all of our lives. She stayed home and raised the kids and took care of the house.

Bev graduated from college a semester ahead of me and got a very good job as an executive secretary with the Coca-Cola Company in Los Angeles. She supported me through the last semester of school and kept working until the birth of our first child, Bob. Bev has always been my greatest supporter and helper and has certainly made a major contribution to our marriage and financial success. She has always corrected and typed all of my papers and letters, and when I retired, she worked with me as a clerk in a convenience store so we could both earn our Social Security quarters and qualify for Medicare.

When I was a young teacher I would often have four or five different jobs during the week. I would teach my regular job, then coach football after school. Then I would teach a night school class and call square dancing one night a week. On Friday nights and Saturday I would referee football games. In other seasons of the year, I was also a gymnastics judge, for which I got paid and I was also a starter for track and swimming meets.

One summer I was a cop for the city of Avalon on Catalina Island. Another time I was a security guard at an atomic energy plant. I also delivered for a drug store on a bicycle when I was a teenager and worked for the Post Office several years at Christmastime. One year, after football season, I got a job through the college as an office boy doing mostly filing in a downtown LA business. This was long before computers. I also worked several years, both day and night, for Sparklett's bottled water company, loading and unloading the delivery trucks.

I was an extra in the movies from the time I was five until I was about nineteen. I was in movies with Bing Crosby, Mickey Rooney, Spencer Tracy, Boris Karloff, Freddy Bartholomew and many others. One summer I was a tour guide for a group in Europe.

Another summer I worked as a farm laborer or helper. We had an acre or two of gladiolas and every morning at 6:00 A.M. one of my jobs was to cut the flowers to be taken to the wholesale market that day. I have also cultivated rows of corn behind a horse. One summer after retirement, Bev and I picked apples in Washington State for the season.

In the Navy, I was an officer and a gentleman by an act of Congress, but I did just about everything aboard a ship except to be captain, executive officer, or engineering officer. I was the navigation officer, in charge of cargo, recreation, the deck and rigging, and gunnery. I was the first lieutenant who is the man in charge of the maintenance and repair of the entire ship except for the engine room.

I also played professional football for three years.

Volunteer jobs, not for pay, include being a volunteer fireman, bicycle tour guide for a group of teens through Europe, a docent in a state park, a nature interpreter in a National park, and serving on many boards of directors. In nearly every organization I joined, I have been elected president or chairman of the board.

There are probably five or six jobs that I have overlooked or forgotten. As I wrote this I kept remembering other jobs I hadn't thought of for years. The variety of jobs has made life interesting. I have been willing to try anything at least once, and then tried to work my way up to something better from wherever I was.

I have learned something from every job I worked and have probably gotten more out of them than I ever gave, but it has all been fun.

Chapter 39

A Memorable Thanksgiving

Thanks to my one-year Fulbright Scholarship, our family traveled to Holland in August 1951. We had an orientation session in Arnheim before starting our school year. There were about 100 Americans in the Fulbright and other programs in Holland that year. By November we were well into the school year and were spread all over the country in various towns and villages where we were assigned. We didn't see much of the other participants from the States except for one or two with whom we had become especially friendly.

The American ambassador to the Netherlands invited all of us to a Thanksgiving celebration. It was held in Leiden, a very picturesque canal city in the midst of acres of commercial flower gardens, one of the oldest Dutch cities and the seat of the famous Leiden University. Leiden is also noted for its fifteenth century Gothic Cathedral of St. Peter. Characteristics of the Gothic style included great height, pointed arches, large beautiful stained glass windows, and flying buttresses.

The pilgrims were refugees from England and moved to Holland in 1608. They settled in Leiden and worshipped in St. Peter's Cathedral until 1620 when they left for America. The tomb of John Robinson, pastor of the Pilgrim Fathers, is in this St. Peter's Church.

Thanksgiving Day broke crisp and clear. It had snowed three or four inches during the night and the countryside was beautiful with its mantle of snow on the trees and bushes and farmlands. They did not plow the streets and there were not too many cars at that time. So there was a hush and stillness throughout the land.

We drove our used Anglia, a British Ford we bought in Paris. Early in the morning we bundled up our two children and set off from Haarlem where all was peaceful as our car didn't make much noise in the fresh snow and there was little traffic or people about in this farmland countryside.

Though a pale sun was shining, it was beastly cold out. There was no heat in the great old cathedral, but at the main entrance there was a large iron stove. As everyone entered, some attendants took a shovel and filled a small stove about the size of a metal lunch box with some live hot coals. Each person took the small stove into church and used it as a foot warmer between their feet. We sat in church all bundled up with overcoats, gloves, boots, mufflers, earmuffs and hats, hovering over our small foot-warmer stoves. We built a kind of tent with our overcoats to keep all the meager heat of the little stoves as close to our bodies as possible. It was probably colder in this great, tall, drafty, stone cathedral than it was outside with the sun shining. The service, fortunately, was fairly short. It included greetings from the ambassador and the singing of some traditional hymns. However, it was a thrill to worship in the same place our Pilgrim forefathers had before they cast off for America and Plymouth Rock.

After the church service, we went to a neighboring restaurant where we had a magnificent Thanksgiving dinner hosted by the ambassador. It included everything typically American, from turkey, cranberry sauce, and sweet potatoes to pumpkin and mincemeat pies. It was a wonderful feast and we enjoyed seeing our friends again.

After dinner we climbed back into our little Anglia, tucked in our full, but tuckered-out kids, and headed back to our hometown of Haarlem as the 100 or so other Americans fanned our to their homes all over Holland.

We have had many memorable family Thanksgivings with children and grandchildren, but that one in Holland was very special and will always be remembered.

Chapter 40

Trauma

Joe and Ann Gray were the best friends we made when we moved to Reseda in the San Fernando Valley. Joe and I both taught at Northridge Junior High School, and discovered that we lived only one block apart in Reseda.

Joe and Ann took us on our first family camping trip to the east side of the Sierra Nevada to a spot called Rock Creek Lake up near Tom's Place on Highway 395. They introduced us to camping, fishing, hiking, backpacking, and all the fun involved in our great High Sierra country . We have spent many, many happy days camping and hiking with them. We give them credit for teaching us all we know about those exhilarating experiences.

After a few years in their Reseda house, the Grays moved into a new home in Northridge that was nearer the junior high school. They had just moved in when we went up to visit them in their new home. They had three children—two boys and a girl—Mike, Kip, and Ellie. Kip and our Bob were the closest in age so were the best of friends, although all of the kids got along well together. During this first visit to their new home, our Bob and Kip were running around in and out exploring the new surroundings. They were chasing each other, as eight-year-olds will do. Bev and I were chatting with Joe and Ann in the family room when Kip came roaring into the room and out the sliding glass door that he slammed shut behind him. Bob came tearing around the corner, not having seen Kip go through the door and close it. As it was a new house and all the windows were spotlessly clean, one couldn't tell whether the door was open or closed. Bob was a quick, tough eight-year-old, so he piled right through the closed sliding glass door, shattering it. He could have been killed, but he was lucky. He didn't have a mark on him except that one sharp slab of glass had come down on top of his left arm, nearly severing it above the elbow. This happened right in front of all the adults sitting in that room. Ann was a registered nurse and I was a Red Cross first aid instructor at that time, so we gave him immediate, competent first aid. I wrapped a towel around his arm, held him in my arms and we headed for the nearest hospital in Northridge. They took good care of him there and discovered that he had severed the radial nerve in his left arm. This is the major motor nerve in the arm and controls the ability to move or raise the arm and hand. Bob could have had a useless left arm the rest of his life. They called in a neurosurgeon and he was able to sew the nerve sheath together. There was nothing they could do about the nerve itself, but they said it might regenerate itself back up the sheath in time.

Bob had a removable splint for his forearm, which held his hand out straight so it wouldn't drop down in a ninety-degree position. He recovered from the accident very well and our insurance paid for the shattered door. We kept the splint on Bob's arm for almost a year and he could do most eight-year-old children's activities with one arm, although he couldn't raise or move his left arm.

In those days I was a National Ski Patrolman at

Vernon still skiing in his eighties.

the Table Mountain Ski Area in the San Gabriel Mountains near Los Angeles. My main purpose in being a patrolman was enabling the entire family to ski free, and this saved us a lot of money for ski tickets for many years. At that time there were many rope tows as well as Poma lifts, T-bars, etc. There were no quadruple chair lifts such as they have today. Bob could ride all of the lifts with his one good arm and his left arm in the splint. He would just place the splint arm on the rope tow and haul himself up the hill, mostly with one hand.

About a year after Bob's accident, we were skiing at Table Mountain every couple of weeks, as usual. We had a small camping trailer we hauled to the ski area to spend the night. Bob came in at the end of the day with a very soggy splint. I unwound the sodden ace bandage that held on the splint to dry Bob out a little. When his arm was free, he wiggled it a little bit and shouted out, "Dad, look, I can move my arm." That was the first time in a year he could elevate his hand. Apparently his radial nerve had regenerated down through the nerve sheath and his arm was as almost as good as new. It got stronger with full flexibility by the following summer.

Later, in high school Bob was a pole-vaulter and gymnast on the horizontal bar, where they do giant swings of their body around the bar, holding on with only their two hands. I would call that a complete recovery from a very serious accident. It was a trauma our family faced together and defeated with complete success. Thank you God for your help!

Chapter 41

Pedaling through Europe

Once upon a time long ago when I was young and foolish, I agreed to lead a group of ten teenagers on bicycles through Europe for a summer. They ranged in age from twelve to seventeen and were to be gone for two months traveling through England, Belgium, the Netherlands, Denmark, Germany, Austria, France, and Switzerland.

The trip was under the auspices of the American Youth Hostel (AYH) which had organized the excursion for us. The AYH is a wonderful organization for travelers young and old. In 1960 I was elected president of the Pomona, California, chapter of AYH. It was a strong group and the Board of Directors decided that we should charter a plane and take a group to Europe for the summer and ride through eight countries on bikes. Although we had only a couple of thousand dollars in our treasury, I signed a contract with a charter airplane company for nearly $100,000 for a round trip to Europe and back. Then we began rounding up travelers. We kept the price under $1,000 per student which included two full months of travel and room and board in youth hostels. We ended up with over 100 students divided into groups of ten with one adult leader for each group. We took off in summer of 1963.

The leaders were made up of teachers, school administrators, nurses, and other people of that ilk. I was principal of a junior high school at that time. We left from Ontario Airport in Southern California where the Reverend Bob Richards, the Olympic pole vault champion whose face appeared on many Wheaties boxes, came to bid us farewell and to tell us to be "good" not "ugly" Americans in these foreign lands. As preparation for the trip, each participant had to be able to travel fifty miles a day on his bicycle with full saddlebags.

I led one group of ten including my own two children. Their ages ranged from our daughter Dee, twelve and a boy, nineteen years old. There were six boys and four girls including one set of twins and our son Bob, age fourteen.

We flew to London and our first job when we got there was to assemble eleven bikes, which we did in a storage yard much like a Bekins' lot. We spent a couple of days in London getting our legs and "seats" set before our two months trip through eight countries.

Dee started her menstrual period in London. I sent the girls into a drug store while the boys and I stayed on the sidewalk guarding eleven bicycles. The girls came out with the largest box of napkins I have ever seen. It was certainly the large economy size. The carton would not fit on any bike so we tore it apart and distributed the contents among all eleven bikers. I'm sure all of the girls were well supplied for the remainder of the summer.

Besides our bike travel we also traveled by ferry, train, subway, and river cruise boats. Trains in Europe travel pretty much on schedule with little layover in stations. Imagine the stress of finding the correct cars, loading all packs and bags, our eleven bikes, and getting ten kids on board before the train pulled out.

Bob Carter, age 14.

Our itinerary and reservations at hostels for the trip were made by the AYH office in New York. Everything worked out to perfection. All we had to do was to make our fifty miles a day to get to the hostel where we were expected for our evening meal.

There were a 100 or more events and experiences I could relate about that summer. We had many flat tires, broken bikes, some illness, and a few accidents, but I'd like to tell you about just one. David lost his passport. As all travelers know, this is pretty critical. We were in Germany and the nearest American Consulate was in Frankfurt, which was not on our route. Fortunately, Dave was with his twin sister Diane, so I sent the two of them off on the train—bikes, packs and all—to Frankfurt to see what they could do. One of the regulations at the time was that if someone could vouch for being at your birth in America, the consulate could issue a replacement or temporary passport. As Diane was the oldest and was born five minutes before Dave, she could swear that she was present at his birth. This was good enough for the consulate personnel so they gave him another passport and the two of them caught another train to catch up with us that evening for dinner at our next destination.

We returned safely all in one piece although there were times when I wanted to kill all ten of them and I'm sure they likewise would like to have killed me on numerous occasions.

The incident that was the most trying to me, however, occurred along the Rhine River. We had spent the night in a hostel in Cologne, Germany, where we had enjoyed visiting the magnificent cathedral that had been repaired from damage received in World War II. I never tried to keep the group in lock-step formation with all ten bikes in a row together. Before we started out each morning I explained our route and destination for lunch and for the end of the day. Then they would travel in groups of two or three as they chose. Our route on that particular morning was an easy one. We had to go only sixteen miles along the Rhine River from Cologne to Bonn where we were to take a steamer up the river to our evening hostel. I emphasized that we all *had* to meet at the steamer dock in Bonn by 11:00 A.M. One of the boys had some bike trouble so I went with him to a neighboring village to find a bike shop and get him fixed up. When I arrived at the dock, I found only about half of our group there. I expected the rest of the group to show up with no problem, but as the time for departure drew near, they still hadn't arrived and panic really set in. I contacted a local policeman who didn't speak any English and was no help at all. I biked around town to the main square and all around, but still couldn't find the missing five members. When the steamer arrived at the dock, smoke was coming out of both my ears, but with great aplomb I put the five kids who were there aboard the steamer with bicycles, packs, and our group tickets for ten people. I sadly waved them goodbye as they took off up the Rhine without me. Then I retraced our route out of the city of Bonn, which was the capital of West Germany at that time, looking for my juvenile delinquents. I finally found them way out on the edge of town sitting in a grassy area writing post cards home and catching up on their journals. I was really fit to be tied and exploded at them. "What are you doing here? You were supposed to be at the dock before 11:00 A.M!" Their answer was that they had seen me leave the main route with the boy with the bicycle problem and they assumed that I was still behind them. I should mention that my own two children, Bob and Deanna were among the miscreants.

Enough recriminations! The next challenge was to get us fifty miles up the river to the next hostel by that nightfall. It was too far to cycle in the time we had. There were no more steamers. What was the solution? One of the requisites for leadership on an expedition such as this was to be able to *improvise* in emergency situations. There was a train along the Rhine in this area, right alongside the highway on which we had been cycling. I discovered a train was due in fifteen minutes, so we raced through the city to get to the train depot in time for the train. To make my morning complete, I caught a wheel of my bike in a streetcar track and had to bail out by doing a couple of barrel rolls across the street. Fortunately, my bike was not damaged and I had only a few scratches and cuts on the palms of my hands where I had broken my fall. We made it to the dock in Mainz ahead of the steamer so we were standing there to greet the other five of our group as they arrived. I gathered my little flock together and in lockstep rode up the hill to our hostel for the night. Smoke came out of the nostrils of the dragon for several days!

When we went up a very steep hill with our fully loaded bicycles, it was okay to get off and walk your bike up over the steepest part. I had no objections to this, and I'm sure most of the kids did this somewhere along the journey.

My son Bob was a skinny little kid, but a very tough fourteen-year-old. He and I had an unwritten pact that we would pedal our bikes every inch of the way, and never walk them over the steepest mountains.

As we were leaving Germany and going into Austria from Munich to Innsbruck, we went over a very steep pass from Oberammergau to Seefeld, a spot where we had skied ten years earlier. I was huffing and puffing over this very steep pass when I was passed by an old German farmer in his truck. He honked his horn at me and as I glanced up, there was my daughter Deanna (twelve years old) in the cab of the truck smiling and waving to me with her bicycle comfortably ensconced in the back of his truck. Dee was a sharp girl and not at all shy. She knew the easiest way to get into Austria! She turned thirteen in Munich.

Chapter 42

Austria

When asked which country is my favorite I generally think of the Scandinavian countries of Denmark, Norway, and Sweden. They all are beautiful much like Wisconsin and Minnesota and they also have lots of interesting sights to enjoy in the major cities. The fact that Beverly is of Norwegian descent may also be a factor.

My other favorite area of Europe is the Alpine region of Austria and Switzerland. When I was teaching in Holland we had a Christmas vacation provided for us so we planned a trip to Austria for the holiday with another American Fulbright family. We decided to drive down in our British Ford Anglia. This is a small compact car about the size of an old Volkswagen Beetle. There were four of us with the two children and also our au pair Reit whom we decided to take along to help care for the kids. Reit was a rather hefty nineteen-year-old Dutch girl. Between us five and all the baggage for each, we were really loaded and packed in the car. We stayed at the Seefelderhof Inn in Seefeld, Austria, just outside of Innsbruck where the Winter Olympic Games were held many years later.

Bev and I were thirty years old at the time and had never skied before, but with this opportunity, we rented skis, boots, and poles and went for it. The ski instructors were mostly Austrian farm boys of the local area who found a profitable sideline for the winter. As I remember, ski lessons were about 50¢ for half a day. We had a lot of fun, learned how to ski down the gentle hills pretty well, and didn't break any bones.

From that smooth beginning in Austria I haven't missed a season of skiing for over forty years and was a volunteer National Ski Patrolman for some twenty-five years. I even skied this year (2001) after my recent quadruple bypass heart surgery.

In 1963 I took ten teenagers bicycling through Europe for the summer on the AYH trip. We covered much of the same area as in our 1952 Fulbright stay . We cycled through Holland, Denmark, and Germany and then over a steep pass from Garmisch-Partenkirchen to Seefeld and down into Innsbruck so we were able to revisit in the summertime the same area our family had visited ten years before.

We cycled all the way across Austria from Innsbruck in the west through Salzburg which is *Sound of Music* country, to Vienna in the east. Although this was through the heart of the Alps, our cycling wasn't too difficult as we were traveling mostly down the river valleys of the Inn, Salzach, and Danube Rivers. Austria is beautiful with the year round snow covered mountains, and the colorful homes and chalets with murals painted on their walls (just like Oroville) and geranium flower boxes in all of the windows.

We visited the famous beer hall in Munich, Germany as well as the place where Mozart lived in Vienna. We stayed in a Youth Hostel in the castle which was seen in the background of the opening scene of *Sound of Music* and the kids explored the entire castle during the night with their flashlights.

A safari to Africa is unique in its own way and outstanding. Australia and New Zealand are far away and certainly special, but after visiting some twenty countries of Europe Austria has to rank on the top for color and interest, and it is a relatively inexpensive country compared to Switzerland and France.

Chapter 43

London

London is one of the great cities of the world like Paris, New York, and other well-known metropolises. I think Paris is my favorite big city, but London must be near the top of everyone's list.

When I took the family to the Netherlands during 1952–53 while I was a Fulbright exchange teacher, we had made friends with some English folks who were married to Dutch friends of ours and they had relatives in Great Britain. When we expressed an interest in going across the channel, they arranged for us to stay with some of their relatives.

Times were still difficult for the British after WWII. I believe they were still on food rationing and many things were in short supply. It was suggested that instead of taking a box of candy for a house gift, we might take food such as butter and eggs, which were plentiful in Holland. We loaded our suitcases with as much as we could carry.

We flew from Amsterdam to London and were met by a chauffeur and a limousine hired by our hosts whom we had never met. He loaded our bags with their precious eggs and other edibles and tucked us in the back seat with a lap robe to guard against their cool English climate. We had never been in a limousine before and it was quite a contrast after buzzing around Europe in our little Anglia Ford and staying in youth hostels.

Our hosts were wonderful people who both worked, but they organized our agenda so we could make the most of our short time there. We stayed about a week and took in all of the obvious tourist attractions we could find. Our first trip to London was the most memorable as our eyes were wide open with wonderment.

Bev and I have always been music aficionados and currently enjoy every program that comes to the Oroville State Theater in our hometown. On our various trips to London since our memorable visit, we were able to see *My Fair Lady* and *Oliver* on the London stage.

Years later, when my friend John Lonsdale and I went to Africa, we had one full day to spend in London between flights. It was easy to stow our bags in a locker and take the underground right from the airport from Heathrow into downtown London where we spent the day. John had discovered a tear on one of his bags so we stopped at a little notions store and bought a needle and thread. On our return to the airport we sat at a table surrounded by our bags while John did his repair work to get us on to Africa.

I feel very comfortable in the great cities like London and Paris and will visit them whenever I get the chance. There is always something new to see as well as the old standbys like the Louvre in Paris and St. Paul's Cathedral in London. I have cycled through both cities without getting killed and have bought and sold a car in Paris, and have walked countless miles in both cities, ridden their subways, and enjoyed their buses and taxis. Won't you join me on the next expedition?

Chapter 44

Yugoslavia

Bev and I took off in our British Ford Anglia and went through Germany, Austria, and Switzerland and then down into Italy where we had not yet visited. This was part of the traveling we did when our family went with me to the Netherlands from 1952–53 for my Fulbright teacher exchange scholarship. While a family took care of the children, Bev and I drove all over Italy from Milan and Venice in the north to Pisa, Florence, Rome, and Naples in the south. We also visited the country of San Marino which is in Italy and then Trieste which was independent at that time. A special highlight for me was to visit Bologna which is the ancient European home of my American fraternity Kappa Sigma.

From Trieste we entered Yugoslavia with our final proposed destination being Greece or Turkey. Of course Yugoslavia has been much in the news in the past few years. Ethnic rivalry is a characteristic of Yugoslav's life. Six major ethnic groups are found there along with several minorities. There are the Slavs, Serbs, Croatians, Bosnians, Albanians, Macedonians, and Montenegrins. In all of these groups there are three major religions, Eastern Orthodox, Roman Catholic, and Muslim.

When we were there it was a Communist country under the dictatorship of Tito. It was the first Communist country we visited and we naturally had more concerns about going there than we had in the many other countries we already visited.

In the light of all the wars, atrocities, and ethnic problems we have seen in the past couple of years, I think we should give Tito a lot of credit for maintaining peace in Yugoslavia for the twenty or thirty years he was in control. Of course he ran the country with the iron fist of a dictator and probably shot anyone who disagreed with his edicts, but he did keep peace among those now-warring ethnic groups.

We found the roads to be in much worse repair than the rest of Europe we had visited and there were more armed soldiers in evidence. Room and board was much cheaper than the rest of Europe and we moved up in class for fewer of our American dollars. One night we stopped at Lake Bled, which was a beautiful resort area where Tito maintained a chalet in the middle of the lake.

Everyone was very kind and courteous to us and we did have a good and inexpensive time in Yugoslavia.

We had been away from the children for nearly a month at that time and as we sat in the deluxe restaurant in our hotel overlooking Lake Bled with the castle on an island in the distance, we had a little conversation about the children and suddenly discovered a great deal of loneliness for them. We decided to cut short the rest of our planned itinerary and hightail it for Holland as fast as we could go starting early the next morning.

When we got to the border the next day about noon there were many soldiers present. English speaking was not quite so easy in Yugoslavia, but we finally understood that there was some kind of a military funeral taking place at the border and all facilities including banks were closed until late that afternoon. I had a considerable wad of Yugoslavian dinar in my wallet as we had expected to stay in that country longer. There was no way to exchange their money into Italian lira, so I took the big wad of bills and tucked it in my socks and we headed for the border barrier as we wanted to be on our way and did not want to hang around for hours to exchange our money.

With our heart rates a little elevated, we made it across the border okay, but when I tried to exchange the money the next day in Italy, we found it was practically worthless, so we took a little loss on their money as our last memory of Yugoslavia.

We didn't waste any time sightseeing, and we set new records for speed on the autobahns of Germany (no speed limits) and across France and Belgium— back home to Holland. Boy, were we glad to see our kids on the beach in Holland!

Chapter 45

Luxembourg

Luxembourg is a small country between Belgium, Germany, France, and Holland. To put that part of the world in perspective, Los Angeles is about 4,000 square miles and Luxembourg is 1,000 square miles. Belgium and Holland are only about two or three times the size of Los Angeles. Driving from one of those small countries to another is a matter of a few hours. Driving clear across Luxembourg is like driving from our home in Oroville, California, to Sacramento.

When living in Holland we had three days off every week so one sunny spring day we decided to go to Luxembourg during this time period. We jumped into our Anglia-Ford one Friday morning and crossed Holland and Belgium arriving about noon in the city of Luxembourg which is the capital of the Grand Duchy. We found a very nice youth hostel and decided to stay there for the weekend. There are several rivers flowing out of that hilly country including the Moselle and the Mass. There was a nice swimming area near a bridge across the Moselle so we took a refreshing afternoon dip diving from a board there. The river was the boundary with Germany and there were armed soldiers across the river on the other bank. I wondered how far I could swim across before getting in trouble or shot at. It made for a very anxious swim.

When traveling independently as we did much of

our lives, we had many unusual and exciting experiences which we ran into purely by chance. Serendipity is a benefit of this kind of travel. This was true in Luxembourg. We discovered that on the Saturday we were there they had scheduled an annual international Catholic festival in honor of St. Vitus. He was the patron saint of handicapped children who suffered from St. Vitus "dance" and perhaps other childhood diseases. Parishes from all of the neighboring Catholic countries had sent busloads of children to this all day event. There was a huge parade all through town with each parish group forming its own unit. There were thirty or forty children in each group and they were holding handkerchiefs with their neighbor on each side. This probably prevented some "sweaty" palms and also gave them more room to maneuver. Then they skipped through the entire parade hopping three steps forward and two backward. They skipped through the entire parade hopping three steps forward and two backward. This gave them a hippity-hoppity gait which would resemble children who were afflicted with St. Vitus dance. We stood enthralled watching this unique parade going by and taking many pictures of this unusual event we had stumbled upon.

This was in 1953 just a few years after WWII and wrecked buildings were still in evidence and most all of the buildings were pock marked with bullet holes as this was an area near the Battle of the Bulge during the war.

It didn't take us long to see all of the other sites of Luxembourg and we visited the large cemetery just across the border in Bastogne in Belgium where so many American casualties from the Battle of the Bulge were buried. It was beautifully maintained by the locals there.

Another serendipity experience comes to mind. When we were visiting in Sydney, Australia, Bev and I got up early one Sunday morning to take a walk around town. We walked over to the famous Opera House which was built right beside the harbor. You have all seen pictures of it in every Australian travel brochure. On that day, to our surprise, all of the Scots in Australia were having a celebration and the courtyard in front of the opera house was full of marching bagpipe and drum corps in their kilts playing inspired Scottish music. I don't have a drop of Scotch blood in me but I get emotional at events like that and I had tears in my eyes as I took pictures of those stirring and colorful bands marching towards us.

Serendipity and Luxembourg we love you.

Chapter 46

Bev's maternal grandmother was born in Norway and immigrated to the United States when she was seven years old. When I was a Fulbright exchange teacher in the Netherlands in 1952–53 I met a group of Scandinavian physical education teachers at an international sports convention in Haarlem and I was invited to teach a summer school class at the Royal Academy for Physical Education in Stockholm.

Getting a paid trip to Stockholm gave us the chance to visit Norway and to visit Bev's grandmother's birthplace. We took a train across Sweden from Stockholm to Olso, Norway. It was through beautiful country with many trees and lakes, much like Minnesota. After enjoying all of the sights in Oslo we set out early one Sunday morning on a bus to Herre the town of her grandmother's birthplace. The bus stopped along the road and dropped off two naïve American babes in the woods with their suitcases in hand where the driver pointed us up a dirt road. There was no town. A quarter of a mile away was a cluster of a few houses so we started walking in that direction carrying our suitcases. Herre is a *tiny* village of perhaps two hundred people. There was no gas station, hotel, motel, café, or McDonalds. As we trudged up the dusty path toward the nearest house a man came to meet us. He didn't speak a word of

English but realized that was what we spoke so he motioned for us to follow him up through the village to a particular house and knocked on the door. A woman came to the door who spoke English. She was Scotch and married to a Norwegian mackerel fisherman named Pederson. She was the only person in the village whose native language was English. She invited us into her home and gave us a cup of coffee as we explained our mission to visit Hilda Thompson's birthplace.

Herre is basically a lumber and fishing village and is a company town as there is a small lumber mill there. She explained that the entire village was going on a Sunday picnic to an island down the fjord in about an hour. There was nothing else to do with us so she invited us to go along with them. The company tug boat had a large barge tied alongside and the entire population climbed aboard the barge along with the two American refugees in tow.

Mrs. Pederson explained to everyone who we were and why we were there and everyone made us feel most welcome.

Some of our most memorable travel experiences have happened by accident or chance and this was one of them

Everyone had brought baskets full of food and drink and there was no shortage of good things to enjoy. They all wanted to hear our story and it was repeated over and over again. Bev's grandmother was alive at that time as she lived to be ninety-four. The oldest person in the village was eighty so no one there was alive when Hilda left to come to the United States but they did know the family name and by the end of the day Bev was a relative to the entire population. The village did have a small Lutheran church and that evening the pastor reported that he had found Hilda Thompson's baptism record in the 1800s

When we returned that evening the Pedersons put us up in their children's room for the night as there was nowhere else for us to go. There was no bus service through Herre on Monday so our host, the fisherman, took us in his mackerel boat across the fjord to Skein a large town where we could catch a train back to Oslo. The boat was open like a skiff or dingy. It didn't have a cabin, but was about twenty-four feet long with an inboard engine. It wasn't luxurious, but it was exciting and a wonderful conclusion to our Norwegian odyssey looking for Bev's roots.

Chapter 47

Gestapo and Fascists

We visited Yugoslavia while Tito was still in power of their Communist regime. That was the first time we had been behind the iron curtain and we had more than a little anxiety about entering a Communist country with which we were not familiar. We were intending to spend about a week there and so exchanged the appropriate amount of money we thought we would need. We did have a very enjoyable time. Yugoslavia was quite inexpensive compared to Italy, France, or Germany and we had some very nice accommodations and meals at modest prices. We had spent quite a bit of time in Italy and we entered Yugoslavia at Trieste and headed for Ljubljana. We spent one night at the lovely resort area of Lake Bled where Tito had a chateau or castle on an island in the middle of the lake.

As I look at a map of that area today I have to take my hat off to Tito. Although he ran a totalitarian communist state with an iron hand he was able to keep the many diverse cultures united under one regime for many, many years. If you look at a map today Yugoslavia has become Serbia, Slovenia, Croatia, Bosnia, Herzegovina, Macedonia, and Montenegro.

Another time we were speeding down the highway in Spain from Barcelona to Madrid when we were stopped by a "Guardia Civil" (civil guard.) They were famous or infamous federal policemen that Franco stationed all over the country and in every village to maintain the power and control of his Fascist regime after the Civil War of the thirties. They were like spies and the Gestapo in Germany during Hitler's time. A peasant could not go from village to village without the proper ID and papers. The Civil Guards wore green uniforms with heavy green ankle-length overcoats and funny hates similar to hats from Napoleon's time. The hats were made of a stiff Bakelite material or perhaps metal. They had a straight up and down section instead of a brim.

A trooper stood in the middle of the road and stopped our car for no apparent reason. I speak little Spanish remembered from my Spanish class in high school. He was hitchhiking and said he wanted a ride into the next town. He didn't ask, he told me! So Bev had to climb in the back seat of our two-door Anglia Ford and he climbed in beside me. We took him about fifty miles down the highway to his destination. I used this opportunity to converse with him in my pidgin Spanish and we got along pretty well. I asked him how he liked his job, what he thought of Franco, and about the economy of Spain at that time. We got along comfortably well, but it is daunting when an armed fascist trooper commandeers your car and tells you to take him to the next town.

When I have been forced to call upon policemen for directions or help I have found them to be of little use. If they didn't speak any English they seemed to be embarrassed and didn't want to be involved with us in any way and just waved us on our way as if to say "Don't bother me." I have found this true of most public employees in most countries. I can remember special incidents in Denmark, Russia, Germany, and France. Included were post office clerks, bus drivers, streetcar conductors and policemen.

We have been fortunate in our travels. We have never had a car accident or been robbed or assaulted in any way. Our contacts with the dogmatic, autocratic, and bureaucratic police and other officials have been disconcerting but painless. Please don't let these little incidents I have recounted here discourage you from exploring this great world of ours.

Chapter 48

Two Front Teeth

Our son Bob was a scrappy, tough and wiry youngster. We had a lot of fun together when he was a little tyke growing up. We had some archery bales of hay that we used to shoot arrows into in the backyard, and we played around a lot together as we were real buddies.

One afternoon we were playing touch, tag, flag, tackle football or all of the above in the front yard of our first home in Reseda. I guess I was running with the ball and Bob made a heroic dive at my legs to tackle me. He was a "go for broke" kind of guy and went for my churning legs. Unfortunately, one of my heels came up and hit him in the mouth knocking out his two front teeth—Wham! As I remember, he cried a little, but not much. He went searching for his teeth and found them in the grass, and finding them was most important to him.

Now, all children lose their two front baby teeth as part of the ritual of growing up. I don't know the exact age at which children are supposed to lose their baby teeth, but I think it was a little early for Bob. They were not loose and he hadn't said anything about them, but there they were in his hand and he was the kid on the block without his two front teeth for quite a long time.

When my dad came to live with us from Missouri we were quite cramped in our first home which was two bedrooms and one bath, so we decided we needed more room for Dad.

We found a nice brand new home in Canoga Park which is located a little further out in the San Fernando Valley of Los Angeles. It had a fairly small sized backyard, but we decided to put in a swimming pool like everyone else in California. We put a nice sized pool which was 20' by 40' and it filled up the entire back yard pretty well.

Our family enjoyed outdoor living and we had a lot of fun in that pool as long as we lived there. Our daughter, Deanna, was a tough, robust young lady about four or five years old when we moved to Canoga Park.

She hadn't learned to swim yet, but loved the pool and had no fear of the water.

She would jump in the water by the side of the pool and as she came up for air she would grab hold of the edge of the pool. As she became more adventurous, she would run around the pool (no running allowed) and as she came to each corner she would jump into the pool from one side, across the corner, and catch the edge of the other side of the pool as she landed in the water. This was a great game and a lot of fun in the water as she didn't swim a stroke.

Unfortunately, she misjudged her maneuver one day and as she came down in the water on the other side of the pool, she was too close and knocked her head against the cement edge of the pool. Guess what? She knocked her two front teeth out on the cement of our brand new swimming pool.

Needless to say, she learned to swim in the next week. I guess I was a delinquent father because I had not yet taught her to swim. Since she was having so much fun jumping into the pool, we didn't see the urgency.

We didn't have any dental insurance and we didn't believe in dentists anyway. If our kids needed extractions we took care of it ourselves.

Chapter 49

Our Kids

We have three children, Robert Craig, Deanna Sue, and Carol Ann. Robert was known as Bobber, Bobby, and Bob. Today we call him Bob, but he goes by Bobby with all of his friends. Deanna was known as Baby Dee, Dee-Dee, and today we call her Dee. Carol is called Carol for the most part, but we often fondly addressed her as Care-Care.

Until the ages of about fourteen to sixteen, Bob and Dee were exceptionally well behaved and mannerly kids. We raised them that way and we were often complimented on their good behavior from all of our friends through those developing years. Bev was a psychology minor in college, and I had enough units for a psychology or counseling minor, even though I was a physical education major and had a football coach mentality. Maybe I raised them as I would a football team. I'll admit to being a strict father, but I hope there was also plenty of guidance along the way.

Unfortunately things really changed about the time they were going through puberty, and they were more than ready to go their own way and leave the "football squad" by the time they were eighteen years old.

Bob was tall and lanky instead of having a chunky physique like his Dad. He was never a football player, but has been an outstanding athlete all of his life. I taught both kids to ski when they were five years old and they were both excellent skiers. Bob was on the gymnastic and track teams in high school. He was a pole-vaulter and a long-horse jumper and high bar man in gymnastics.

When he grew up, Bob became a world-class ski speed racer. This is going straight down a measured and timed course with no turns in a tuck position. Bob has gone 109 miles per hour. Compare this with putting your hand out the window of a car when you are traveling at 70 miles per hour. Bob's buddy, Steve McKinney, held the world record at 124 miles per hour on skies.

Bob also became a mountain climber of some renown. He has climbed El Capitan in Yosemite Valley many times, and still made a climb recently at age sixty. He is an expert hang glider pilot and has flown all over the West. He was on a Mount Everest expedition where they attempted to climb to the top which they did not accomplish, but they were the first in the world to climb high up on Everest and fly off in a hang glider landing on a glacier further down the side of Everest. His friend Steve McKinney led this expedition. Steve has since been killed in an automobile accident.

Bob was a professional ski patrolman at Squaw Valley for several years. One of his jobs there was to go out early in the morning and throw sticks of dynamite off of the top of ski runs to knock the cornices or overhanging snow off the tops of the runs. This experience led Bob into his life's career establishing a blasting business in Truckee, California, where he has been successful for many years. His main helper these days is his son Taylor who works with him whenever he is not in school. Taylor enjoys the work too, and may take over his dad's business when he is out of school.

I think: Bob should write his own book of his life. He has done a number of very special things.

Deanna was a good athlete also. She was a strong skier and won a Presidential Fitness award in high school for exercising. She was a very attractive and popular girl in high school in Pomona, and was selected as a princess of the Homecoming Court when she was a senior. I remember inviting Dee and the queen and all of her court as guests at our Optimist Club luncheon during this special occasion.

Dee is very sharp intellectually, and has worked at many jobs and for many companies during her life. Regardless of her job title, after she was in a new job for a few weeks, she was the most capable worker in the organization and was ready to take over and run the whole business. She was not aggressive or pushy, but was ready to receive a promotion and organize and run the entire company.

In later years she has developed into an excellent counselor and guidance person and has been a leader in organizations dealing with spousal abuse, domestic violence, drug and alcohol abuse, and other personality problems. Aside from being an outstanding counselor and advisor, she has moved to the administrative top of the organizations in which she has been involved.

Dee was the only family member who hiked the entire John Muir Trail with me, 225 miles across the top of the High Sierra from Yosemite Valley to the top of Mount Whitney. She was a strong, solid companion who carried her load of food and pulled her weight every step of the way. I would recommend her as a hiker to anyone.

Along the way, Dee has been an outstanding

mother to three daughters, homeschooling each of them through high school into a life of motherhood themselves. Now she is a grandmother of two being raised by two of her daughters. She is a "Grandmother Supreme!"

Bob and Dee were born sixteen months apart and have had a close relationship all of their lives.

Our third child, Carol Ann, was born nine years after Deanna and was a joy to the entire family. We noticed she didn't develop as the other two children had and had a neurological workup done on her when she was about three months old. Unfortunately this proved her to be severely mentally retarded with the

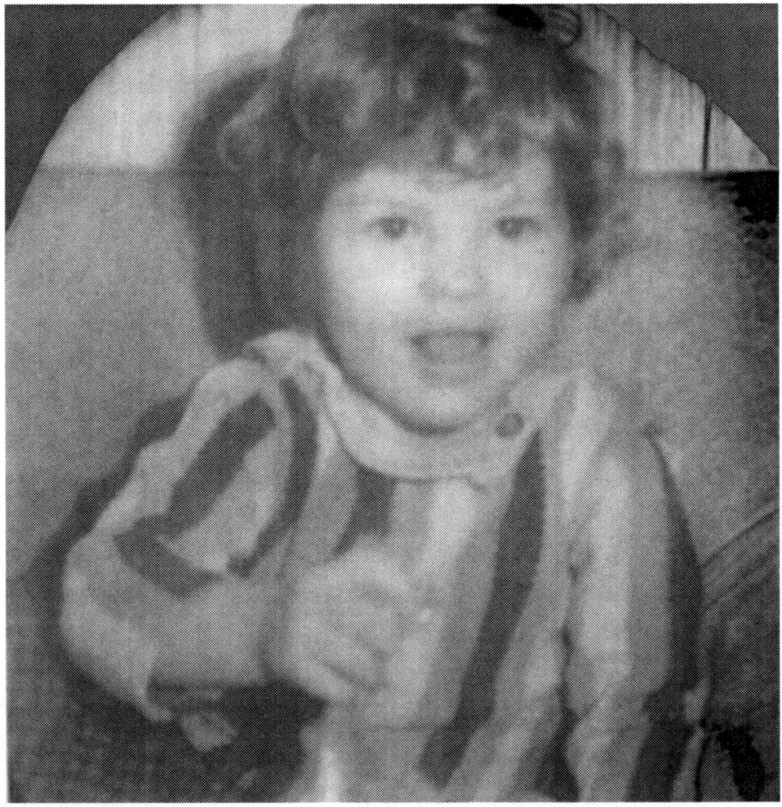

Carol Ann Carter

prognosis of her never walking and a recommendation that we place her in a care facility. We don't know the cause as Bev had a normal pregnancy with no particular problems at birth.

We kept Carol at home with us for seven years. Bev fed her every mouth of food she ate and changed every diaper for seven years. Her brother and sister loved and adored Carol as did we all and we all doted on her. She was a very pretty child and did not look retarded in any special way.

Chapter 50

Bouquet Canyon Camp School

Los Angeles City Schools give tests and establish waiting lists for all teaching and administrative jobs which are used for three to four years. When I graduated from college, I took two tests in the PE field. There were about 350 candidates who took each test. When the lists came out, I was number one on one list and number two on the other list, so I got a job right away. I graduated on a Friday in February and started teaching the next Monday.

After eight or nine years of teaching, during which time I had gone to summer school and night school to earn an administrative credential—I was ready to look for that kind of position. I took the LA vice principal's exam and again, there were about 300 candidates. I came out about fifteenth on the list and probably would have been picked within the next two or three years, but I was impatient, so I started looking outside of LA for an assignment.

We had two children by this time and I always had three or four extra jobs to support the family as my wife stayed home to raise the kids. One of my extra jobs was teaching at juvenile hall and probation camp schools at night. Through that contact I heard the county was opening a new camp and needed a principal, so I applied for and received that job as my first administrative position.

There were about 100 boys in camp for everything from murder to grand theft auto, assault, robbery, burglary, etc. I left the LA School District and started with the LA County Schools as principal on July 1, 1957.

The county Probation Department ran the camp and the county special schools ran the education in the camp. The two agencies dealt with the same clients—the boys assigned to the camp. In some camps relations were so bad between the two organizations that the principals and camp superintendent didn't even speak to each other. I was selected to change this condition in our new camp. That principalship was my first administrative job.

We did develop the best relations of any camp-school in the county and were a showcase school. It was really pretty simple. I made a point of going over to the probation side for a coffee break every morning at ten. We discussed all of our mutual problems and solved them in this informal setting. This experience motivated me to write my doctorial dissertation on "Relationships Between the Schools and Probation Department." It is interesting to note that the same bad conditions exist today in Butte County between juvenile probation and the county schools office.

Our new school was being constructed so we were placed in an old CCC (Civilian Conservation Corps) facility left over from the Depression. When the first lonely boy arrived at school, I handed him a paintbrush and told him to start painting all the old abandoned buildings. He did a good job and took great pride in what he had done. As more boys arrived in camp, I gave them paintbrushes and added to our crew. They painted the entire school and also took pride in their work. As I remember, we didn't have any graffiti appear after their hard work.

While there, I hired three or four male teachers and we carpooled together from the San Fernando Valley each day out to the camp. They were all good teachers and did an excellent job with the boys.

When each boy arrived in camp, I gave him a battery of tests to determine his level in the fundamentals of education. Then I placed him at that level of competency regardless of the grade that he had been in at school. We had plenty of materials at all levels so the students were able to make fast progress from where they were on arriving at camp. I emphasized counseling with all of the staff so we had few discipline problems with anyone during the day. The boys stayed in camp from six months to a year and I feel that we really brought them ahead in their school-work, maybe two or three years in that time. We did PE with them and played volleyball in our limited space. I remember badly spraining my ankle playing with the boys one day, and I was on crutches for two or three weeks recuperating. I got a good razzing from the boys for that episode.

I enjoyed my year at Bouquet Canyon and felt that I made an impact on the County Schools program and the County Probation Camps. I also found a subject of interest to me for my doctoral dissertation. Although this was my first real administrative job, as I was a principal of a school, I recognized that if I stayed in this prison-like setting for very long I might be considered out of the mainstream for other educational administrative jobs. So even though I was very happy there I kept my files active at USC, had my resume ready and my eyes open and continued to explore other opportunities within the main educational stream. I stayed at Bouquet Canyon for only one year.

Chapter 51

Optimist Club

I got a job as vice-principal at Emerson Junior High School in Pomona in 1958. It seemed to me I ought to join a service club. When I was a teacher in a classroom or on a gym field I obviously couldn't get away for lunch off campus. I don't know where I got this idea in my mind, but I was aware of service clubs in the community and I thought it was beneficial for a couple of reasons. One, it is good to have the schools represented in the community. It is good public relations for the schools. Two, service clubs do positive things to make a town a better place in which to live.

At this point in my life I was very happy with my place in life. I had a good education, a good job, a successful marriage and family, and I wanted to give back to the community that had provided so much for me.

My principal Lyn Johnson was a member of the Rotary Club so that particular club was out, but he obviously had a positive attitude toward service clubs. I approached him with my idea and he agreed that it was appropriate for me to join a club. I was new to Pomona, but he had been in the area for a long time and was well acquainted in town. He checked around and found a friend he knew in the Optimist Club who was willing to sponsor me and take me into the club. His name was Art Smithen and he owned and operated a small one-man neighborhood grocery store. Art came by school every Monday morning at 11:45 and picked me up for lunch. The Optimist Club was a strong well established club of about fifty men who met weekly on Mondays at noon. Art was a sweet man older than I was and not an aggressive proselytizer for the club. After I had a perfect attendance for about a month, he had still not asked me to join, so I asked him one day, "How does one become a member of this organization?" That speeded things along and soon I was a fully paid-up member of the group.

The motto of the Optimist Club is "Friend of Youth" and a major part of their effort is in support of youth football and baseball teams, Boy Scout troops, 4-H clubs, etc. A special emphasis is on Junior Optimist clubs directed toward junior-high-age boys. The Pomona club had never had a Junior Optimist club. Soon after I joined the club they approached me with the idea of starting one. This came naturally as I was now an Optimist and my job was vice-principal of Emerson Junior High. I gave the proposition some thought and said, "Okay, if you will let me do it my way." They agreed, so off I went. I had an ulterior motive in the back of my mind. I always figured if you can kill two birds with one stone so much the better. For members of this Junior Optimist club, I picked the ten boys in our school who were sent to my office the most for disciplinary problems, i.e., the most troublesome boys in the school. We formed a club, had weekly meetings after school and once a month I took them on Saturday outings to interesting places in Southern California such as Knott's Berry Farm, Disneyland, the park, the zoo and other exciting places.

These were not "bad" boys, but were just not getting enough personal attention in their lives. Some other Optimists and some mothers helped with transportation and supervision on our Saturday expeditions, and I did a little subtle counseling during our weekly meetings. When they got all of this attention from these Optimist male models and the vice-principal of the school, their whole attitude at school changed. They stopped being sent to the office for discipline, their grades improved, they became my friends, and the Pomona Junior Optimist Club was a huge success that was written up in the Optimist International magazine.

I have been an Optimist for fifty years now and it has been a very important part of my life. Most of our social friends have been club members and I have enjoyed making a contribution to the communities in which I live through the club. The highest honor in Optimism one can receive is to be "Distinguished." The main thing to achieve to win this honor is to build a new Optimist Club.

In my Optimist Club I was Man of the Year in 1959. This resulted mostly from forming the Junior Optimist Club at my school. I was a Distinguished President of my Optimist Club in 1961 for starting a new Pomona Evening Club. I was a Distinguished Lt. Governor of Zone 17 in the Pacific Southwest District of Optimist International that included all of Southern California from San Diego to Bakersfield in 1967, for building a new club at Cal Poly University, Pomona. When I was superintendent of schools in Blythe, California, I was president of the Blythe Optimist Club.

When I retired and we moved to Oroville, California, I started the Oroville club and was its first president. In 2002 I formed the Chico Optimist Club and was again a Distinguished Lt. Governor.

One can readily see how much the Optimist Club has meant to my life. It has given me much pleasure and enjoyment and a tremendous feeling of accomplishment.

I should mention that my wife Beverly and I have been married for sixty-one years as this is being written, and she has been at my side and my greatest supporter through all of these years. Fifty years ago the club was for men only. They had an unofficial auxiliary called Opti-Mrs. Clubs. Beverly was president of the Opti-Mrs. Club in Pomona and now that the Optimists have gotten smarter and taken women into the clubs, she is a member with me in the Oroville club.

Chapter 52

Going by Airplane

We have talked about my journey through life by various means: bicycles, boat, train, etc. We haven't said much about airplanes. Everyone who reads the daily paper is aware of the many problems of flying these days, late and cancelled flights, lack of service, employee strikes, crashes, lost luggage, poor parking facilities, long lines, extra charge for bags, etc.

As a child I was never particularly interested in airplanes or flying. I didn't dream of being the Red Baron of even Snoopy. I first joined the Marine Corps in WWII and then transferred to the Navy not the Air Corp.

However when I was forty years old an unexpected opportunity presented itself. I became the superintendent of Sierra High School District in Fresno County. My predecessor had been a flight instructor in WWII and had been at Sierra for twenty years. He owned an airplane and had put in a dirt airstrip behind his house. He sold me everything he had accumulated over the twenty years of his service and which I naively bought. He tried to sell me his plane too, but I reneged on that. I had no use for it as I couldn't fly.

As I settled into my new job my wife, Beverly, was still in Los Angeles trying to sell our house there. As I had an airstrip in the backyard and long lonely evenings, I began to think of something positive to do. I didn't see any harm in taking some flying lessons so I enrolled in a ground school course and began flying down at Fresno Air Terminal. I got along pretty well as I had lots of quiet evenings to study, and after about ten hours of flying time I soloed and eventually got my private pilots license.

This opened a whole new vista of excitement, a new way to travel, and a lot of new adventures for me and the family. We ended up owning two airplanes, a Cessna 150 and a 172. We kept them in the backyard and flew from the dirt strip, a "Band-Aid" as Bev called it. I had the best of two worlds as I learned how to get in and our of small "Band-Aid" strips but learned at Fresno Air Terminal which was a major airport with control tower and radio procedures.

We had a lot of fun for the next five years. We flew in and out of Mexico and from San Diego to SFO and Sacramento and Las Vegas along with many dirt strips in between.

Bev is basically acrophobic and uneasy with heights. She wasn't at all interested in learning to fly or even to accompany me in our small plane, but good sport that she is she went everywhere with me. She learned just enough about map reading and the instruments to be a real troublemaker. She would look on the chart and see that the two peaks we were headed for were at 6,000 feet. She would glance at the altimeter and see that we were at 5,500 feet. Her palms would get sweaty and she would poke me and indicate the "problem" she saw ahead and wanted to know what I was going to do about it right then? Of course I did have a plan of going through the valley between the two peaks where the elevation dropped to 4,500 feet. Hakuna Matata, which is Swahili, means "No Problem"!

There were many thrilling and funny stories we could tell about our flying experiences but if you asked each of us to tell about the same incident you wouldn't know we were on the same continent let alone in the same plane. Her stories are much like a Steven King novel, sheer terror and catastrophe. I, on the other hand, had a lot of fun trips accumulating some 500 hours of flight time and I did become more proficient as I gained more experience.

Interestingly, both our planes eventually were crashed and wrecked. Scouts' Honor, I had nothing to do with it. I had sold my interest in the first plane to my partner and one day commuting from Auberry to Fresno with his wife he ran out of gas and landed in a field. They walked away from that with some cuts and bruises but the plane was totaled.

Later while we were on a trip to Alaska our other plane was securely tied down (we thought) at our home airport. A desert funnel cloud came along, picked up the plane, broke the tie-downs, and crashed it into the ground on its nose. It was "totaled." I sold it for half its value for parts and junk and it was towed away on a truck. Sad day!

I could go on and on and regale you with other stories, but I would just like to say flying one's own plane is another fun and exhilarating way of getting from one point to another on this great planet of ours.

Chapter 53

Blythe—Colorado River

I was superintendent of schools in Blythe, California, for a couple of years. Blythe is located on the Colorado River in the low desert. We enjoyed living there where we had a boat and did a lot of water skiing on the river as well as fishing for striped bass and trout. Bev was interested in and quite involved with golf and played weekly on the lovely course they had in Blythe. She also played in many tournaments with other women's clubs. It was an active, healthy life for both of us.

My assistant superintendent was Harry Roberts who had been there a few years before I arrived. He and his wife Olga became our good friends and showed us the ropes in life on the river. We did a lot of boating, skiing, fishing, and hunting together. Quail, dove, duck, and geese were all plentiful along the river and it was fairly easy to limit out on most birds.

Harry and Olga were also members of the Blythe Volunteer Fire Department, so Bev and I joined that group. It was good to be part of a volunteer group such as that in the community. I had been a volunteer fireman in Fresno County, but this was a new experience for Beverly. We went to all of the training sessions, but were real rookies.

We did go to quite a few fires as Blythe is an isolated city with the nearest towns to us about 100 miles away, with Needles on the north, and Yuma on the south and the great California desert on our west all the way to Barstow.

We were often called out for desert brush fires a long way from home. One day we were at a fire far out in the boonies, almost halfway to Yuma fighting a "forest" fire which was desert brush. We were going to be there all day so headquarters decided to send us some lunch. They called on Beverly to drive a truck with sandwiches and drinks out to the men fighting the fire. She started out all alone with directions to turn here and there on country desert roads. Some of the roads were dirt or gravel and soon Bev was lost. She did have a radio in the truck and she was communicating with home base for further directions, but she was pretty well frustrated with the whole thing and thoroughly lost. When she was through talking on the radio she would drop the microphone onto her lap and continue on her way. Now, she had been married to me for twenty-five years and had heard most all of the cuss words in the English language from me many times over so she was cussing aloud to herself, "Why in the blankety-blank did they send a rookie like me out on this assignment all by myself." She went on and on. Little did she know that her microphone was picking up all the mumbles and all her private expressions of disgust were being broadcast all over Riverside County. Bev earned quite a reputation in the county fire community. However, she did eventually find the fire and crew and delivered the lunch as directed, which was most welcome. Though she was tempted, she didn't resign from the fire department over this incident, but continued with her good volunteer work.

Blythe is about 100 miles from the Mexican border, and migrant workers are often legally brought into the state to work the bountiful crops of this Southern California area. One day a rattletrap old bus was bringing a group of workers into our area. The driver was a Mexican with little ability or experience as a bus driver. He was way out in the boonies on a back road and came to a spot where the road made a ninety degree right turn with the road ahead ending in a dead end. The driver missed the turn completely and went straight into a ditch about thirty feet deep. I don't know how fast he was going, but the bus ended up in the bottom of the ditch, landing on its nose in a vertical position. All of the seats broke loose and the passengers landed on top of one another crammed into a cluster at the front windshield of the bus. Everyone on the bus was killed. They called the volunteer fire department to the scene. Three young firemen and I volunteered to go into the bus and get the bodies untangled. They were in a mixed up jumbled mass, piled on top of one another in the front end of the bus. We had to pick an arm or a leg and untangle that body, then pass it out of the door to other waiting firemen who passed the body from man to man up the steep twenty-foot cliff to the road. The bodies were laid out side by side along the road. There were twenty-eight dead bodies, men and women, including the bus driver, in that accident. We worked in that bus for hours untangling one body at a time. It was a horrendous, emotionally draining experience, the worst of my life. When we finally got the last body out and came up to the road for fresh air, the chief sent the four of us home immediately as he knew we had given our "all" in that massive carnage. Of course the other firemen had to stand by and transfer the twenty-eight bodies stretched out on the road into the ambulances and vans that came to cart them away. I'll never forget that day of volunteering.

I had my airplane with me in Blythe moored at a small private field in town. It was fun flying up and down the river exploring the countryside. We were in Riverside County and the county school's office was located 170 miles west of Blythe in the city of Riverside. We had countywide meetings frequently to which, as superintendent, I was expected to attend. It was a great convenience having my own airplane, as I was able to fly 170 miles into Riverside Airport where someone from the county office would pick me up for the meeting.

Another advantage of having an airplane I found during geese-hunting season. It was difficult to know exactly where on the river the flock had settled in for the night. It was not always in the same place, so sometimes hunters would wander in vain looking for the geese. Others would just happen to stumble on a huge flock. I remember one time, in hoping to improve our odds, Harry and I went up in my plane to scout the area. We went up and down the river to see where the geese were settled. This system worked pretty well. We found them, went back, landed the plane, and picked up our guns, and went to the geese with good success.

We spent many hours on the river water skiing, and we were always looking for new stunts to try. Someone discovered that a round piece of plywood measuring about thirty-six to forty inches in diameter was a handy and fun piece of equipment to play with. One could stand on it while being pulled behind the boat, making 360-degree turns on it, and stand backward to the boat while being towed. Then we took a three-foot wooden stool with us, not attached to the disc, and we would set the stool on the disc and

Vernon water skiing on his head.

attempt to stand up on top of the stool while underway. It was "doable."

I was a gymnast in college and a gymnastic coach
for two years at Marshall High School, and remember, I was a PE major. This all led to my attempt to

perform tricks. I had done about every stunt we could think of while behind a boat on a rope. One day I thought of something new to try—a headstand on the disc while being towed. I made many tries in many ways resulting in many falls. Finally I figured if I turned around with my back to the boat and placed my hands with the handles of the rope about two or three feet apart on the middle of the disc, I could bend over, place my head on the back of the board between my hands, and do a headstand while being towed by a ski boat at about twenty miles an hour. After lots of tries, with many failures, lots of falls, and lots of fun, I made it. As far as I know I'm the only person to have done that stunt. Many of my buddies tried it all summer, but nobody made it. What one won't do for a little fun and attention!

The teachers in Blythe hadn't had a raise for a couple of years and were rather disgruntled with my predecessor superintendent. I was pretty good with figures and was very careful and conservative with

The Laney family, co-owners of our boat the Colorado River.

the budget, but I found I was able to work out about a six percent raise for the teachers the second year I was there. Of course this action made me very popular with the teachers. They loved me!

We were very happy in Blythe. We enjoyed living there and the teachers were delighted with me, but I was always looking for a better position with more money. I had my papers on the "open file" at USC and knew when there were better jobs available. I made several applications for new jobs over the years and went to several interviews, but I wasn't always successful. There was plenty of competition for all of the positions, and often twenty or thirty applicants for each opening.

There was a good opening in the metropolitan area of Los Angeles County for which I applied. A couple of school board members came out to Blythe to interview me, and I was offered the position of superintendent with the Wm. S. Hart Union High School District in Newhall. The advantages for me were a move from the hinterlands of the California desert to the big downtown area of metropolitan Los Angeles County. I had been earning $23,750 in Blythe, and was offered $36,000 in the Hart district. This was a nice step ahead for us in 1974.

Chapter 54

The John Muir Trail

There are many ways of traveling: airplane, cruise-liner, auto, bicycle, and yes by foot. Sightseeing by walking hiking, or backpacking is a wonderful way to go for those who are physically fit enough for the kind of experience they are planning.

The John Muir Trail is one of the great experiences and undertakings for those who are able. It stretches 225 miles from Yosemite Valley to the top of Mount Whitney at 14,495 feet across the backbone of our great Sierra Nevada here in California. It is a part of the greater Pacific Crest Trail that runs from Mexico to Canada across California, Oregon, and Washington.

For those of us who live in Oroville we should be aware of the Pacific Crest Trail in our backyard. If you have driven to Reno via Highway 80 you have crossed the Crest Trail in the vicinity of Boreal Ridge Ski Area or right near the crest of the highway at Donner Summit. Hikers cross there and walk without crossing any major road until they come to Highway 70 near Belden.

Our family has backpacked on, across, and around the John Muir Trail for many years. My wife, Beverly, has done about seventy-five miles of the trail, and both of our kids have hiked a lot of it.

One summer when I was forty years old, many,

many years ago, I had some extra time on my hands and felt that was a good time to tackle the entire trail in one trip. As usual when I plan some of my more adventuresome expeditions I could not find anyone my age who was interested or fit enough for such a trip so I had to turn to a younger generation. I recruited my daughter Deanna, who was nineteen years old, and her friend Trisha and her brother Bobbie. My sister had four boys who were all good hikers, and two of them also joined up with us. Brad, her oldest, was a great hiker who has since done most of the Pacific Crest Trail through Oregon and Washington by himself. His younger brother Phil was fourteen at the time and this was his first big hike. This made us a group of six.

Beverly, as usual, was our efficient liaison and transportation and supply resource. Our plan was to hike the entire John Muir Trail of 225 miles in thirty days. This would be done in two sections of two weeks each. That would mean we would hike only about seven and one-half to eight miles a day on average. We were not out to set any all-time speed records. We could carry all of our food for two weeks at a time before needing to re-provision. My regime for this trip was for me to get up at 6:00 A.M. and start the fire for hot water for breakfast and then get the kids up. Breakfast consisted of Tang and instant oatmeal and coffee. We would break camp and be ready to hit the trail by 8:00 A.M. We could hike about two miles an hour with full packs, food and all, so we could hike eight miles by noon and have our day's work done. Lunch consisted of packages of soup, crackers, and dried hard salami which keeps very well, and Kool-Aid.

We could spend the afternoon fishing, exploring,

reading, swimming, sun bathing, or resting before dinner and bed. We caught lots of trout and ate every one supplementing our diet.

My sister's four boys are all over six feet and big people. Brad and Phil were especially good football players. Today Phil is six foot, six inches, and weighs 240 pounds. When he was fourteen he was about six feet and weighed 180 pounds or so. His coordination had not caught up with his body size so he was like a wild bear in camp. Every time he walked near the fire he knocked a pan over or tripped on a piece of wood or fell in the fire. He fell off of every rock he had to scale and fell in every steam he had to cross. Every time he had a catastrophe upsetting the entire camp, I came out with a huge bear growl "arrgh," "arrgh," and that was Phil's identification. He remembers his uncle Vernon and those incidents to this day.

Beverly dropped off our intrepid crew in Yosemite Valley one bright and sunny summer morning and we were on our way. Two weeks later we had to take a boat ride across the lake to reach a road and there was Beverly right on schedule to retrieve our weary bodies. She took us home where we had hot baths, food, especially ice cream and milk and where we loaded our packs again for the second half of the trip. We went back in at Florence Lake and picked up our trail.

The trail ends at the top of Mount Whitney, but then you have to hike fourteen miles more (downhill) to Whitney Portal. From there it is about ten miles to the nearest town which is Lone Pine on Highway 395. There are lots of cars and traffic at Whitney Portal so we found a nice fellow with a big truck in the parking lot and he was kind enough to take us down to Lone Pine.

We called Brad and Phil's dad as the plan was for him to drive up from Los Angeles and pick us up. This is a four- or five-hour trip and we got him on his way in the afternoon. Then we found the best restaurant in Lone Pine and spent the next few hours eating until he arrived. We had the best things on the menu and then kept ordering ice cream, apple pie and Pepsi.

Not everyone is physically able to undertake a trip such as this, of course, but thousands of people climb Mount Whitney every summer and hundreds hike the entire John Muir Trail every year. However, it was a great feeling of accomplishment and success for our little family group aged fourteen to forty. It created a special bond between Deanna and me and I am likewise very close to my sister's four boys. We are all proud we made that hike when we did.

Chapter 55

The Grand Canyon

The Grand Canyon is truly one of the natural wonders of the world. Anyone who drives up to one of the lookout points for the first time and sees that magnificent expanse spread out before him as far as the eye can see has felt the marvelous impact of the scene. Of course, there are some people who jump out of their car, take one look, jump back into their car and head off to the next stop—Las Vegas.

Bev and I first visited the canyon on our honeymoon in 1947 and we have been back many times since and I have developed a real affinity for its vastness and grandeur. We have lived in both Blythe and Needles, California, both of which were close enough for an easy one day trip to take friends, visitors, and tourists for their first look.

Being hikers for many years and knowing there were trails from the top of each rim to the river in the bottom of the gorge was a challenge we could not ignore. On one of our early trips Bev and I hiked about half way down to Indian Garden where there is water and a campground. I, of course, had to hike to the bottom and back out "because it was there."

After I was retired and living in Needles in 1977 I had made friends with a retired mortician who had not done much hiking nor did he engage in much physical activity, but he was game to give it a try.

His daughter Johnnie went with us. We hiked down the South Kaibab Trail which leaves from Yaki Point on the South Rim. The trailhead at 7,000 feet is 7.3 miles from the Colorado River and Phantom Ranch which are located at an elevation of 2,400 feet. It took us about five hours to walk the steep, rocky switchbacks that wind down along several ridges. Walking downhill, dropping more than 4,000 feet in elevation is physically rigorous. It is tough on the thigh muscles and the toes which are jammed into your boots on every step. We carried full backpacks with sleeping bags, air mattresses, food for just one day, a stove and a gallon of water per person.

We made the trip down alright and spent a peaceful afternoon beside the river and camped in the open by Bright Angel Creek which comes down from the north rim. The next morning we got an early start and took off together across the foot/mule bridge. We each had our gallon of water with us. I have found when hiking that each person should set his own pace rather than going in lock step in a group. We were hiking up the Bright Angel Trail which is longer (nine miles) but a little more gradual.

Shortly after crossing the river Chuck, my friend, was moving slower than I so after a conference I decided to move on at my pace and his daughter, Johnnie would stay with Chuck at his pace. You can't get lost on that trial and it isn't difficult but takes determination. They do haul many casual day tourists up the trails on mules frequently.

Having had lots of experience hiking I plodded along the trail and reached the top in about five hours. I rested, had lunch and plenty to drink and looked anxiously down the trail for Chuck and Johnnie. As time passed I became more concerned and sent water, cookies, and fruit down the trail to them via other hikers who were starting down. Finally I spotted two little specks moving very slowly far down on the trail. I jogged down to them and relieved Chuck of his pack so he could get to the top. He was really beat as it had taken them about nine hours to make it out. He collapsed in the back of his pickup and I drove us home to Needles. It was a memorable trip and a great hike.

Following that hike I dreamed of going through the entire canyon on the Colorado River in a rubber raft. I was able to fulfill that dream in 1979 with the Sanderson Company, one of the best rafting companies. I went with a group of twenty people, all strangers to me, on two rafts. We met and spent the night in a motel in Page, Arizona, then left from Lee's Ferry the next morning. We stopped and visited all the sights along the way including Navaho Bridge, Nankoweap Canyon, Red Wall Canyon, Elves Chasm, Deer Creek Falls, Havasu Creek, and Lava Falls Rapids, which is a class 10 rapids. We wore life jackets at all times in the rafts and were wet all day long. We went through many, many rapids and had to hold on tight. We camped on beaches along the way and slept in the open on cots. You do shake your shoes out every morning. One time I did find a scorpion under my cot when I awoke and we found one rattlesnake. The food was excellent, the guides were great fun, and the trip was exciting and thrilling. We policed each camp and brought out every scrap and cigarette butt we hauled in. The company provided porta-potties and all excrement was hauled out in barrels stored in the bottom of the rafts. This was another memorable and fabulous trip I was privileged to have taken.

Elderhostel is a great organization for seniors over fifty. I especially like their service programs where volunteers work on worthwhile community projects. A few years ago I left Oroville to participate in an eco-system restoration project around Grand Canyon Village. We collected seeds, removed alien plants, and planted native vegetation and worked in the nursery. I enjoyed working hard for a week helping to maintain the Canyon Village. When my young granddaughter was asked where I was going, she said, "Grandpa is going to *fix* the Grand Canyon." I hope I did a good job because I love that wonderful place!

Chapter 56

Mexico

There are probably few people in Oroville who have not been to Mexico, at least across the border to Tijuana. We are fortunate to have a foreign country so close at hand and so easy to visit. It comes with a completely foreign language, different money, and a culture quite different from ours even though we do have the advantage of many Mexican-American and Spanish-speaking people in our communities.

Our family has spent a lot of time in Mexico over the years. We have enjoyed many summer vacations water skiing at Estero Beach just nine miles south of Ensenada on the Pacific Ocean side of the Baja Peninsula. It is a wonderful place to stay right on the beach with trailer hook-ups, showers, great skiing and is overall quite inexpensive. On another trip we traveled another 100 miles south to San Quintin for fishing.

We have flown our plane to Ensenada and to other fishing villages on the east side of Baja on the Gulf of California. We have pulled our trailer down to Hermosillo on the mainland and over to Kino Bay on the east side of the gulf. Some of the best fishing we have ever experienced in our lives was out of Kino Bay.

I would like to share with you one particular trip we made long ago. We have some "character" friends named Joe and Ann with whom we have camped and hiked in the High Sierra and on the John Muir Trail, and we have also traveled to Australia, New Zealand, Fiji, and Tahiti with them. They like to go the "cheap route" and that always makes the trip more adventuresome. Early in our relationship they heard of a Greyhound bus trip nonstop (sixty hours) from the San Fernando Valley to Mexico City for practically nothing. In Mexico the Greyhound is called the Chihuahence. We agreed to this expedition, so the four of us met the bus early one morning in San Fernando. In an American Greyhound we tooled down through LA and I-15 to San Diego and then over I-8 to Yuma and across Arizona and New Mexico to El Paso, Texas, where we entered Mexico and changed to the Chihuahence in Juarez. Now that's a long drive in itself from LA to Texas but we were young and full of energy and we were still in the good old USA so everything was going pretty well all things considered. The Chihuahence had a toilet in the back, the upholstery was not quite so plush, it ran pretty well, but the roads were really bumpy and full of chuckholes.

The stops along the way were very primitive, maybe just a little local store along the highway. Nothing even to compare with perhaps a McDonalds let alone a Denny's. The restrooms were found around in back, and often out in the open, just a ditch. We decided not to drink any water along the way so we survived on beer directly from a bottle at each stop. We slept sitting up in the seats like our Greyhounds or the old coaches on trains. As we were getting pretty tired by now we did manage some sleep at night. There was one double seat in the back of the bus by the toilet. Ann lay down on that seat and was sound asleep when we hit one particularly big bump and it catapulted her clear out of the seat and onto the floor in the aisle.

We went down through Chihuahua, Torreon, Guanajuato, and into Mexico City more or less all in one piece. It was a sixty-hour nonstop one-way trip. We got a very nice hotel and spent a lovely week seeing all of the sights such as the volcanoes, the floating gardens, the university, Diego Riveras' murals, etc. and did have a fine time. However, all four of us suffered a bit from Montezuma's revenge before the week was over, but it didn't slow down our sightseeing activities very much.

One can fly to Mexico City and enjoy one of the great cities of the world, but then you would miss the fun of a bus trip on the Chihuahence.

The trip home was much the same but we were hardened passengers by that time so it passed pretty quickly. It was wonderful to hit a nicely paved I-10 when we got back to El Paso.

Coming home we stopped for a toilet break in El Centro, California. All of the stops were very short, maybe 10 or 15 minutes. The bus was ready to go and Ann hadn't come out of the bathroom yet. Bev and I were yelling at the driver to wait, but Joe said, "She'll be along" so we drove off without her. She didn't even have her ticket with her. We went all the way to San Fernando without Ann, but she came in on another bus an hour later. They are still married!

Joe and Ann spend about six months a year every winter in Mexico. They pull a trailer and camp along the beach somewhere. They don't bother with trailer parks or camps. They like to *rough it!* We don't travel with them anymore.

Chapter 57

Leadership

Let's look in the old dictionary first. Leadership is the office or position of a leader or the capacity to lead. To lead is to guide on the way, especially by going in advance or to be first in the group or in the race.

It is difficult to define the qualities of the great leaders of the world. Their qualities are as different as they are unique individuals. Jesus, Mahatma Ghandi, Martin Luther King, Jr., Stalin, etc. The presidents of the United States were all leaders of our country, but some were better than others. I think that Abraham Lincoln is considered the number one president nowadays.

I am not considering myself in any class of comparison with the great leaders of the world, but as I look back on the events of my life I seem to have had some qualities of leadership built in there somewhere.

First let's look at the negatives. I never became an Eagle Scout. I was a Life Scout, next to an Eagle, but I never made that final step. I have regretted this lack all of my life and have always given Eagle Scouts special credit. They certainly had leadership qualities as well as many others. I think this stage of my life—at age thirteen or fourteen—was the first time I thought for myself and about the importance of setting goals in life. I realized that almost anything in life is attainable if one sets incremental goals and sticks to the job ahead. I have always been goal oriented and have achieved most of the goals I had in mind.

I was never captain of a football team. Most captains were voted in by their teammates. I think I was a late bloomer and many of my qualities of leadership developed a little later in life. In junior high school I was too young and immature to even consider running for student body president, but at Oxy I did run but was unsuccessful. I was still young and immature politically and was overreaching my abilities at the time, but the seeds for later successes were being sown.

Now, to make my basis for some positive leadership traits I may have possessed or acquired.

I was skipped a half a grade in the sixth grade along with Marilyn and Rose. The teachers must have known our test scores and the promotion would indicate that we were somewhat above average intellectually and academically. When I went to Bancroft Junior High I felt that I was a very average person and student both academically and athletically. Due to the "skipping" I was younger both physically and emotionally than most of my classmates. Being skipped at that time was one of the worst things that could have been done to me and I have rued it all of my life, but that's another story.

When I was going into the ninth B grade we moved back to Kansas City. I guess Mother and Aunt Julia were not getting along too well at that time and Mother had had enough of being the scullery maid so she decided to move back to Kansas City, Misssouri after about eight or nine years of living with Uncle Jack and Julia. I don't remember her telling me many of the details.

When I started at Central Junior High School in the ninth grade I was still pretty average academically, but I had suddenly blossomed into a superstar athletically. I guess there was a basic difference between California and Missouri climate-wise, health-wise, and maybe sunshine-wise. For each sport during the year, the PE classes were divided into teams. First, captains were elected by the class, and then the captains chose their teams. It was the old-fashioned system where the best players were selected first and the little fat kid or the skinny kid with glasses was chosen last. I certainly don't approve of such a system today, but they obviously didn't know any better then and I did respect and admire out PE teacher, Mr. Cross. At any rate, I was selected a captain of every team for every sport all semester long. I think we won most of our games with me being the star and some evidence of this was written up in the school newspapers and I still have those clippings today. We had an indoor swimming pool and went swimming once a week. We didn't wear swimming suits so fifty naked little junior high boys were in the pool all together. We had a swimming meet at the end of the semester and I set an all-school record in diving and retrieving an object. I wonder if it still stands? I doubt it. The coach also selected me to be a standby lifeguard during our times in the pool. They didn't have any guards there and the coach was the only person in the place with clothes on so he couldn't go in on a rescue. I think I pulled out a couple of kids who were going down for the third time. These experiences in leadership in PE were my introduction into being considered a leader by my peers and by the coaches too.

I graduated from junior high in January, midterm, and went across the football field to Central High School. My dad, mother, and sister attended my graduation or promotion. Dad lived in Moberly, Misssouri, at the time and was remarried to Alice his former secretary.

In Central High they had intra-mural boxing after school. They did not have boxing in California schools, so I had no previous experiences in boxing, but I was tough and willing to learn. I guess we had some instruction and learned by sparring with friends. Once a week we had a series of matches with a referee who declared the winner. I must have had a big punch since I knocked down everyone I ever fought even up through the Marine Corps and in drunken crawls, bar fights, etc.

It seems that whenever I joined a group and they got to know me they seemed to see some qualities they admired or respected and they eventually picked me or asked me to be the president or leader of their group. I don't know what these particular traits might be but I think I have always been faithful and loyal to any group I have chosen to join. To keep the record straight I will try to list as many as I can think of.

In high school I was elected to the student council in my senior year, a late bloomer.

In college I worked my way through the chairs of my fraternity and was president twice, once before WWII and again after I came back as a veteran. I was elected president of the Associated Men Students (AMS) which was a pretty high honor, next to being student body president. In my junior year I was selected by the college (I don't know how) to Tiger Taps which was a group of about five outstanding men in the college for their senior year.

When we opened Sun Valley Junior High in 1950 I was elected the first president of the faculty of some forty teachers. We were all new to the school and didn't know one another before. Why did they pick me? I was just a young PE teacher?

I was a volunteer National Ski Patrolman for about twenty years and was elected leader of our ski patrol a couple of times.

In Pomona we joined the local chapter of the American Youth Hostels and I became president of the chapter. I joined the Optimist Club in Pomona and worked my way through the chairs and was elected president of the club where by meeting certain goals I became a "Distinguished" president. Then I was elected lieutenant governor of a zone and became "Distinguished" there too. I was also an Optimist Club president in Blythe. I was a "Distinguished" secretary/treasurer of the club in Needles and was charter president for two years when we formed a new Optimist Club in Oroville.

Since coming to Oroville in 1988 I have been treasurer of the Butte County Historical Society, president of the Bidwell Bar Association, and on the board of the Gleaners. I was appointed to the board of the Feather River Recreation and Park District. I then had to run in a public election, the first time in my life, and though I was opposed I won with 81 percent of the vote. I have been elected chairman of that board for the past two years.

None of these offices are particularly vital or earth shaking but they demonstrate a pattern over my eighty-five years of life of some qualities of leadership that have appealed to groups I have been associated with. I don't know what those qualities are specifically. I know I have always been willing to serve my fellow man and my companions in organizations. Maybe many people are shy, but I am not. If one is willing to serve, I guess it is easy to be selected. I know I have enjoyed the experiences along the way and it has always been enjoyable for me to serve. I don't think I'm ready to change.

Chapter 58

Professional Career

In 1940 when I was seventeen years old and a senior in high school, my hero and model was my football coach Meb Schroeder. He had gone to Hollywood High and was a graduate of Occidental College. He was a fairly young teacher and my idol. I wanted to grow up to be a high school football coach and teacher just like him.

He got me a football scholarship to Occidental so I was able to achieve that first professional goal. I seem to have set goals for myself as I made my journey through life. Fortunately, they were realistic and reachable. As I reached one goal successfully, I set another goal in its place to continue my trek.

I graduated from Oxy at midterm on a Friday in February 1948 and started my first job as a teacher the following Monday. I was head football and gymnastic coach at Marshall High School in the Los Angeles school district and a full-time PE teacher. The chairman of the PE department was Cecil Zahn, a USC graduate who was another mentor for me. His advice was to continue my education right away. He encouraged me to take a graduate course at USC during my first summer vacation, which I did.

After two years at Marshall, I opened a new junior high school, Sun Valley, and was the first faculty president there. I also became chairman of the PE department. While there I took a year's sabbatical to be a Fulbright exchange teacher in the Netherlands which is described elsewhere.

On my return, I transferred to another new junior high school, Northridge, as a PE teacher. I spent one hour a day as health coordinator for the school where I worked with the school nurse. This was my first sub-administrative job, but it went on my resume.

During this period I had been taking classes at USC in all of my spare time, and had earned an administrative credential. I discovered there was an opening for a principal of a new Los Angeles County Probation Camp School so I applied for and received that position—my first authentic administrative job.

I spent a year at Bouquet Canyon but was always looking for a way to move ahead to a better position in my career.

I heard of an opening for a vice-principal at Emerson Junior High in Pomona. I was accepted for that position and served for a year when my principal, Lynn Johnson, moved up as principal of Pomona High School.

I applied for the position of principal of Emerson, but was turned down by the superintendent who didn't feel that I had enough experience. That faculty, however, felt that I had done such an exemplary job on their behalf the previous year, that they went to bat for me and convinced the superintendent to appoint me as principal.

I served as principal of Emerson for nine years and turned it into the best school in the district. My two children went to neighboring Marshall Junior High. There was a weak principal there, and for five years the superintendent had been asking me to transfer to that school to straighten it out. I said no to him for four years, but finally agreed to the switch. After nine years at Emerson, the PTA and faculty gave me a surprise "this is your life" party as a send-off.

While at Emerson, I had continued my education at USC and received both a masters and a doctor of education degree.

I worked at Marshall for one year and did a pretty good job of straightening out some of the things that needed attention. With my doctor's degree, however, I was still looking for advancement. The next step would be a superintendency. I was finally appointed superintendent of the Sierra Joint Union High School District in Fresno County. This was the richest district in the state of California. It was in the foothills of the Sierra Nevada that contained several huge electric power plants from the water runoff which were taxed to support this small district with few students.

I spent two years at Sierra and then went to Cal State Los Angeles University as registrar and admissions officer to try my hand at higher education. Cal State had 25,000 students at that time.

From Cal State, I went on to become superintendent of the Palo Verde Unified District in Blythe California, where I stayed for two years.

In 1974 I became superintendent of the Wm. S. Hart Union High School District. That district was named after an old time Hollywood cowboy movie actor who had a ranch in that area. He was before the time of Tom Mix, Roy Rogers, and of course John Wayne.

When I was superintendent it had become a large district in Los Angeles County including the communities of Saugus, Newhall, Canyon Country, Valencia, and all of the surrounding area. We also provided the educational programs for the large prison nearby.

I spent twenty-eight years in my professional career as a PE teacher and coach and whatever else ensued. I retired from that career at age fifty-two. I never considered that I had any other career, but I did continue working at many other jobs as I had all of my life. I spent six summers as a National Park ranger naturalist.

Beverly and I counted up our pesos and figured we could make a "go" of it, so we bought a double-wide mobile home on the banks of the Colorado River in Needles, California, and spent the next eleven years of our life water skiing, catching fish, enjoying the view and seeing the world as we continued our journey.

Chapter 59

Retirement Needles

In 1976 we decided to retire. I had worked at my professional career for twenty-eight years and had gone as far as I could go. I was superintendent of a large school district in Los Angeles County, and there were no other goals that interested me to continue my professional journey.

I felt that I had finally completed my professional journey. There were still a lot of things we wanted to do, new experiences ahead of us, places we wanted to see, and other challenges along the way. I felt it was time to end this phase of life.

We had thoroughly enjoyed our life along the Colorado River during our time in Blythe, and Bev, especially, liked living in the desert, so we were drawn in that direction. I didn't want to go back to a town where I had formerly worked, but Bev had enjoyed Needles, California, when she had visited up there to play in golf tournaments. Needles was located on the river, about 100 miles north of Blythe. One weekend we decided to take a look at the area. We liked what we saw and found a nice mobile home park, Rainbo Beach Marina, right on the river. The lower section of the park at water level was used mostly for travelers, overnighters, weekenders, and winter residents. There was a cliff about twenty feet high and on this bluff the permanent mobile homes were situated with a beautiful view of the river. There was only one lot available on the front row along the top, so we put up a deposit and reserved this spot. We then went to a mobile home factory and ordered a new double-wide home to be built for us and installed on our spot in the park.

The land was rented, so we didn't have title to the property. This proved to create a problem later on, but we didn't know that at the time. The rent was dirt cheap when we started, $60 a month, which was a real bargain.

We did all of the pre-planning for about six months, and were prepared to move in on July 1, 1976, as June 30 was my last day of work. The mobile was supposed to be completely set up, ready for occupancy by that time.

We had a crew ready to help us move in. I drove the largest U-Haul available filled with all of our worldly possessions. Bev and my sister Shirley drove our car followed by our helpers. Upon arrival, we found the mobile was not ready for occupancy. I got on the phone and soon had a crew from the factory come out to finish the hook-ups despite the fact that it was the Fourth of July weekend. It was necessary to get motel accommodations for ourselves and our helpers for the weekend while our house was readied.

We found life in Needles at Rainbo Beach to be all we had hoped it would be. We made many new friends with the regular permanent residents, and the season visitors who came south for the winter. We became acquainted with a group of Canadian snowbirds from British Columbia who had been coming to Rainbo for several years in the wintertime to escape the severe weather in Canada. We had many special friendships with this lovely group of Canadian retirees.

We bought a new boat in Needles and the "livin' was easy." The California Department of Fish and Game stocked the Colorado River with trout three or four times a year, and the truck always dumped their load at our boat ramp for the Needles area. Rainbo Beach was a couple of miles upstream from downtown Needles, so the hatchery fish would make their way downstream toward the town. Of course, this made the fishing red hot in front of our house for a week or so. It was like shooting fish in a rain barrel.

Striped bass were also plentiful in the river. The fish made their way up and down the river to spawn just below Davis Dam which backed up Lake Mohave, near Bullhead City. With all the bass and trout so readily available, we always had fish in the freezer.

At that time, our place was the newest, the nicest, and the largest in the park so it became the headquarters for many cocktail parties, luaus, and fish fries. Bev was known as the "hostess with the mostest." She has always been an excellent cook and could really do a job on striped bass with a special beer batter recipe she had. We often had twenty or thirty friends in for a fish fry dinner.

Occasionally I would swim back and forth across the river for some extra exercise. The Colorado River was a couple of hundred yards wide through Needles, and had a current of about four miles an hour. I would walk upstream to the edge of Rainbo property to start my swim and the current would take me a couple of hundred yards downstream as I crossed. Then I would walk back upstream on the other side until I was above our park and swim back and land right at our boat ramp.

We spent eleven years in Needles and enjoyed living there even though we never spent the summers at home. The temperature can reach 110 degrees in the summer and is often over a 100 degrees for a month at a time. Therefore, we became snowbirds in reverse and traveled north for the summers. We had a truck and trailer outfit that was quite comfortable. We covered all of Oregon and Washington, and then made our way into Canada. Many of our snowbird friends were from a town just across the border called Abbotsford, which is a few miles east of Vancouver. We would park our rig in a trailer park, and enjoy the entertainment and hospitality of our Canadian friends for a week or two. Then we would take off and explore most of British Columbia, visiting Prince George and Kamloops and even the little town of Vernon over near Glacier National Park.

One summer we drove the Alcan Highway all the way to Alaska and traveled most every mile of paved road in Alaska. The report on that trip will follow in a later chapter.

Chapter 60

It Was a Dark and Stormy Night

Our daughter, Deanna Russomano, had our first granddaughter, Shanti Grace, on April 27, 1977. Shanti was an unusual name out of the hippie '70s, but she was also named "Grace" after Bev's blessed mother, Grace Gillett, whose birthday was likewise on that same day. Shanti was born in Edison, New Jersey.

We had put on the wedding for Joe and Dee in New Jersey the previous year. We drove back there along with my sister, Shirley, and our son Bob flew in for the occasion. The wedding was sparsely attended, but the reception following the wedding was a gala, crowded event.

When Dee was pregnant with her second child in 1979, they were living in Fresno, California, in a second-floor apartment. Bev and I were in our retirement home in Needles, California, on the Colorado River. Needles was about a six-hour drive from Fresno and we were on the alert for the baby's arrival. One evening Dee began to feel pangs similar to her first birth, which was a five-hour labor, so she phoned us in Needles and told us to hurry. It so happened that we were having dinner with some guests we had invited when the call came. We abruptly left everything, including our guests, with instructions on how to use the dishwasher and lock up the house. We jumped in the car and took off for Fresno. Dee's experience that night proved to be a false alarm so everything quieted down. We decided to stay, however, until the baby arrived since it would likely be "any day now." It took two more weeks of waiting and we had a good visit with them.

On the night of the big event, Dee's cousins Brad and John Grindrod and a coworker from LA, were driving a moving van full of furniture north. They decided, unexpectedly, to stop and see Dee. This is the only time they ever did that. Dee prepared dinner for all of us in their fairly small apartment. As she was cleaning up after dinner, she began to feel labor pains again. Dee had arranged to have a midwife and a doctor who specialized in home deliveries attend the birth, so she called them both around eight o'clock.

It so happened that that night was one of the worst storms in Fresno history. There was a tremendous downpour of rain and hail with all the streets and underpasses flooded. A tornado touched down at the Fresno Air Terminal. The midwife got stuck in a flooded underpass and had to call her husband to pull her out. The doctors, both husband and wife, also had a terrible time dodging flooded areas and skirting difficult spots to get across town to attend the birth.

Cousin John was only nineteen years old, but very interested in the event and wanted to photograph the entire process. Cousin Brad had some cold symptoms, so we thought it best to keep him away. He wasn't interested anyway, so he and his coworker went out and slept in the moving van.

Deanna had a short and easy labor with her first baby so she was getting along fine, just taking it all naturally. Since it was awhile before medical personnel showed up, Bev and I were on deck expecting to help Joe deliver a baby at any moment. The baby's head had crowned and we were ready for whatever circumstances occurred next. There was still no medic in sight on this dark and stormy night.

The midwife was the first to arrive at the very last moment. The two married doctors followed a few minutes later. The wife decided to take charge and delivered the baby very normally.

Kendra Iam Russomano was born at 11:20 P.M. on February 19, 1980. Dee had been in labor for only three hours. By that time, all the dishes were washed and put away from dinner, and all the guests had found a place to sleep, along with Kendra and Deanna, who were resting peacefully.

Chapter 61

Volunteering

I have had a good life since I have been grown and able to think and do for myself, and make my own decisions. Somewhere along the line I had a feeling that I should give back to the communities in which I lived and which had been good to me.

One of my volunteer efforts was to join the Optimist Club that I have written about elsewhere. The Optimist Club is one of the four major service clubs in the world. The service club movement started around the beginning of the twentieth century with the concept that successful professional men could form an organization with a goal to perform voluntary functions to make their hometown a better place in which to live. I have been an Optimist for fifty years how and have thoroughly enjoyed every minute of its volunteer activities.

When I was in Pomona I joined the local chapter of the American Youth Hostel Association (AYH). This was mostly a group of young bicyclists who went on fifty-mile trips around the countryside on weekends. I eventually became president of the local chapter. During that year AYH sent one hundred young people, in groups of ten with an adult leader, cycling for two months through Europe. I took my own two children with me along with other youngsters. This was one of the most exciting trips of my life. All of the adult leaders of the AYH were volunteers, no one was paid.

When I became superintendent of the Sierra Joint Union High School District we lived in a house the district owned, located on a main highway of the Sierra foothills. It was in the small community of Auberry, California,. in Fresno County. The Volunteer Fire Department building was right next door to our home. There was a loud siren that sounded whenever there was a fire. Since we were always awakened and aware of every fire, I decided I might as well join the Fire Department. I was sure to be one of the first to report at every fire call since I lived right next door to the station. I was accepted in the department and attended all the training sessions as well as every fire that occurred when I was at home and heard the summons. I served for two years during our stay in Auberry and learned a lot about firefighting.

When I became superintendent in Blythe, California, my assistant superintendent, Harry Roberts, was already a member of the volunteer department, so, with his encouragement and my previous experience in Auberry, I joined the volunteer department there. Bev also joined, as Harry's wife Olga was a member and took Bev under her wing as a sponsor.

Uncle Jack and his two brothers, Ross and Jim, were all Los Angeles City firemen and after their retirement, became fire chiefs with the Army and the Air Force. Therefore it was most gratifying to me to follow the family tradition by finally becoming a volunteer fireman.

When we moved to Oroville in 1987 we slowed down from the hectic travel program we had been on for eleven years. This was really retirement. We settled down in a nice custom home we had built, and joined the new community where we now lived. We have been in Oroville for twenty-one years as of this writing.

Upon our arrival in Oroville, I wanted to learn all I could about our new hometown and Butte County.

Lake Oroville was created by Oroville Dam which is part of the California State Water Project. The Oroville Dam was completed in 1967 forming the lake with 167 miles of shoreline. A visitor center complex, atop Kelly Ridge where we live, overlooks the lake and dam. The Oroville Bidwell Bar Association is a voluntary group that assists the park rangers with the operation of the visitor center and all of the dam facilities. After considerable training about the California Water Project and Oroville Dam and Lake, one could become a fully qualified docent at the visitor center. Docents are volunteers with substantial knowledge on the subject who provide information to visitors and guests. I soon became a docent with the Bidwell Bar Association.

After a couple of years of service as a docent, I became president of the association. This association has an annual Bidwell Bar Day, a Christmas program, and provides volunteers for the front desk in the Visitor Center to aid the rangers and give other assistance as needed.

Another organization I felt would give me insight into my new surroundings was the Butte County Historical Society, an organization that maintains and develops a record of the history of the entire county. It is a venerable organization from which I learned much of the history of the area. After several years of service to this organization, I became their treasurer.

Bev and I have visited many of the great art museums of the world such as the Louvre in Paris, the Prado in Madrid, the Rijks in Amsterdam and the

Hermitage in St. Petersburg, Russia. I have always enjoyed art and had a great feeling of esteem for the masters, but I never felt I could paint anything. However, with the help of a snowbird friend from Montana, Jay Gilbert, I achieved my first oil painting at the age of sixty. Since then I have finished a number of paintings and sold a few.

When we first came to Oroville there was an Art League in town which I joined. It was a voluntary group whose purpose was to support an interest of art in the community. That organization was made up mostly of older ladies who had been painting for many years, and it finally terminated.

About five years ago a new art organization was formed called ART, Artists of Rivertown, whose driving force was a friend of mine, Freda Flynt. I was a charter member of that organization which has been doing an outstanding job of promoting and showcasing local art all around Oroville.

I have always enjoyed teaching both young students and adults, as teaching was my chosen profession. The Butte County Library has a strong literacy program that teaches youngsters and oldsters who have difficulty in reading. I saw an announcement in the local newspaper where there would be a training session for literacy tutors. This sounded like it was right up my alley so I attended their orientation meeting. The organization and training was outstanding, and something I felt quite comfortable with, so I joined their group. I have been tutoring now for about fifteen years at the library. I have had students from fourteen to sixty years of age and I have successfully helped all of them learn to read or improve their reading skills. This program has been a source of real joy to me, and given me a feeling of satisfaction. Helping someone learn to read, I feel, is one of the greatest voluntary activities one could undertake.

One day I read an announcement in the local *Mercury-Register* newspaper of an opening on the Board of Directors of the Feather River Recreation and Park District board (FRRPD) and that applicants could attend a special meeting to apply. As a physical education major with classes in recreation, and an interest in recreation and outdoor activities all my life, I felt like I might be able to make a worthwhile contribution to the district. I attended the orientation meeting, was interviewed by board members, and was selected and appointed to fill the vacancy on their board. I ran for election twice and was re-elected by large majorities. I served as vice-president and eventually as president of the board, serving for eight years before I resigned for political reasons. I felt that I made a significant contribution to the district during my eight years of service, and helped provide fun and recreation to the citizens, and especially the young people of the city of Oroville.

Beverly and I together ran a campaign to approve a Benefit Assessment District that placed a ten dollar a year assessment on every home in the district. It is most difficult to ask people to increase the taxes on their homes and properties, but we were successful and won the election by a 51% to 49% plurality. Bev and I placed 100 signs throughout the district, "Yes on Parks," and took them all down after Election Day. We were lucky. We won!

We joined the Unity Church in Oroville recently and rather than being "go to church on Sunday members," we wanted to become more involved. We had been supporting this small church financially for a number of years, and as a result had been receiving their monthly bulletin informing us of their activities. They have a nice small chapel with property surrounding the building so there is considerable maintenance involved in caring for the facility. They hold a monthly work party on a Saturday to trim the bushes, rake the leaves, and hoe the weeds. I had been helping them several times a year on these workdays when I didn't have a conflict with other obligations.

When we joined the church there was an opening on their board of directors. As I had been on many boards before, I volunteered to join their board and was accepted. As it turned out, the job of recording secretary went with the position, so I really had more responsibility than I wanted or had planned on. I found that the liturgical and idiosyncratic local terminology was foreign to my ears, and my hearing which had been diminishing for many years, made it impossible for me to do a good job. This resulted in numerous corrections on the reading of the minutes each month, so the rest of the board graciously accepted my resignation after six months of trial. I still do my clean-up chores every month and we do enjoy the fellowship of a fine group of new friends.

I have been program chairman of the Optimist Club for several years. It is my responsibility to obtain a speaker for each of our bimonthly meetings. The speakers can be of general interest on any subject or circumstance, or keep us apprised of activities and events happening in Oroville.

A year ago a speaker was Janice Titensor, president of the PAWS (Promotion of Animal Welfare Society) of Butte County. PAWS was established in 1981 and is a nonprofit organization whose mission is to provide low-cost spaying and neutering for pets of low-income families. PAWS strives to lower the dog and cat over population in Butte County. Janice is an inspirational speaker whose heart has been with the PAWS philosophy since she was a teenager. She convinced me that this was an organization worthy of my support, so I joined with them. I not only ended up on their board of directors, but also help out in any way I can. They have a large thrift shop whose profit supports the veterinarian program, and I have clerked there. I also propagate plants and flowers and donate some twenty-five or so a month to the thrift shop for sale.

Occasionally I transport an animal to a veterinarian for medical attention. It is a pleasure to support the large number of animal lovers who donate hundreds of hours to the welfare of dogs and cats.

Another worthwhile organization in Oroville is the Gleaners. As the name implies, they glean unused food from various sources and distribute it to the needy in the community. The Gleaners have a large warehouse in town where they accumulate donated leftover food and give it to the needy organizations and individuals. I joined with them several years ago and spent many hours laboring in the warehouse. As has been my pattern, I ended up on their board of directors.

I formed the Oroville Optimist Club in 1997. The Optimist Club is a volunteer organization whose purpose is to enhance its local community in any way that it can. Some of my activities with the club are reported elsewhere.

One of our major voluntary efforts has been the Adopt-a-Highway program. We were assigned a two-mile stretch of Highway 70 on both sides of the highway. Our responsibility was to clean all of the papers and trash from this area once a month. Cal Trans provided us with hard hats, orange vests, gloves, and plastic bags to carry out our responsibilities. I was chairman of this project for ten years. We had a dedicated crew with four past presidents including myself, and a couple of other members including my wife Beverly, all were most loyal participants for the ten year period. In addition to our regular crew, we had youth groups and friends who joined us occasionally. I should mention two very special people. Bonnie Evans, a neighbor across the street who had no affiliation with the Optimist Club other than being our friendly neighbor, was a loyal worker who rarely missed a session in three years or more. In my literacy work at the local library I met Lynn Rich who was an Americorps volunteer with the library. As a friend of mine, and as part of her Americorps program, she also was a dedicated worker on our Adopt-a-Highway crew. The Optimist Club was happy to give these two admirable people recognition in the form of a plaque at one of our club meetings.

Unfortunately, since Bev and I were not getting any younger, and as we had difficulty recruiting more club members to our crew, the club decided to abandon this project in 2008. The trash is there now for the jailhouse crew and Caltrans workers.

Life has been good to me on my journey. Although I started somewhat at a disadvantage with the early divorce in our family, my course has been steadily onward and upward. I have enjoyed helping those less fortunate than I and hope that my efforts have helped ease their way along their paths.

Chapter 62

Habitat for Humanity

Besides traveling to new places I also enjoy trips where I can perform a service and give something to the people of the community I am visiting. I have taught English in Indonesia, worked on reforestation in the Grand Canyon, and participated with Habitat for Humanity in Yakima, Washington.

This Habitat was in conjunction with an Elderhostel service program. I had never spent time in Yakima and was interested in getting to know central Washington better. We stayed in their community college dormitories during summer break. Since their football team was involved in summer practice, the cafeteria was in full operation and the food was not only plentiful but excellent.

Chico and Oroville have an active Habitat for Humanity program. Habitat is an international program best known because President Jimmy Carter swings a hammer in it. I have always been proud of Jimmy because he is the first "cousin" Carter we have had in the White House.

The families who acquire the finished houses must put in many hours of "sweat" labor in construction to earn their houses. Most of the labor is donated by volunteers such as myself and many of the building materials are also donated which brings the cost down very low. Low interest rates are arranged for these families so many people can enjoy and pay for their first homes as owners.

Habitat is a most worthwhile program and a lot of fun besides. About twenty of us seniors signed up for a two-week stint in Yakima. We were from sixty to eighty-five years old including both men and women. There were jobs anyone could do under the supervision of a foreman or contractor. The eighty-five-year-old woman, for example, worked in the office. Most of the time I was there we installed a lot of drywall as well as other jobs. We worked on three different houses. I am not a skilled craftsman but I have a strong back so I was able to carry one-half of the 4' x 8' sheets of dry wallboard or plywood. I could handle one end, but I was always looking for a partner or two to carry the other end into the house where we were working. If anyone should happen to drive up in a truck, I would grab him and ask him to "give me a hand with the other end of this please." We somehow got the job done. At one point another fellow and I were standing in a bathtub installing some drywall board on the other side. We were chatting away and discovered that we were both graduates of USC, he with a PhD and I with an EdD. We thought we should write a letter to the alumni society of USC indicating how two of their doctors had finally made good, standing in a bathtub together, pounding nails.

I would like to touch on another aspect I learned from this volunteer experience, I am a member of the Oroville Feather River Recreation and Park District board of directors and we are very interested in developing our wonderful river all the way through downtown Oroville from the Highway 70 bridge to the Nature Center with special emphasis on the River Bend area which the district owns.

While I was in Yakima, Washington, doing volunteer work I learned a lot about the town. It is located on the Yakima River which likewise flows through the middle of their city. I have also spent considerable time in Spokane, Washington, where the Spokane River flows through its downtown area. Both of these cities have highly developed park areas all along their rivers through town and they are most proud of them as well they should be. One of the first things they show off to visitors to their cities is their beautiful parks along the river. The banks are all covered with lush green grass with bike trails, jogging trails, playground areas, etc. In Spokane I attended weekly concerts in the park which were heavily attended by people sitting on the lawn on blankets.

I thoroughly enjoyed the Yakima Habitat experience and felt that I was able to make a real contribution to its progress. I also learned a lot about colorful city-river parklands and enjoyed our early morning walks through the dew before breakfast. The experience of observing Yakima and Spokane development helped me with planning ideas for Oroville. The Yakima citizens were justly proud of their river land park and we visitors enjoyed being in it in the early morning.

Painting

I never painted anything in my life until I was sixty. I was never one to write on bathroom walls or scribble on my desk at school. At some point I used to try to draw airplanes, but they were pretty primitive things.

For a while in high school, my homeroom teacher was an art teacher and we used to meet for fifteen minutes a day in her room. I was more interested in the girls in the class than the artwork on the walls. I did the required course in music appreciation, but I never took art appreciation in high school. I had no experience with any of the fine arts in college either.

When I was a Fulbright exchange teacher in the Netherlands for a year I began to take an interest in art. By that time as an adult I had read some books about art and had developed quite an interest in art even more than music. I had no natural talent in any of the fine arts. I never tried to draw or paint anything and I couldn't carry a tune in the proverbial bucket.

However, as we visited nineteen countries in Europe during the Fulbright year, I took advantage by visiting all of the great museums. In later travels I have visited the Hermitage in St. Petersburg, Russia, Museum of Modern Art in New York, and Gauguin's in Tahiti. We have also visited other, less well-known museums around the world as well as many great palaces and castles.

During these more mature years I developed an appreciation for artists and their art. I have read many biographies of artists such as van Gough, Gauguin, Pizzaro, etc. and find them exciting.

When I retired as a school superintendent at age fifty-two we moved to our first retirement home in Needles, California, on the banks of the Colorado River. We made many new friends and met many snowbirds from the North who came to the sunny California desert for the winter.

We filled our time playing golf, fishing, partying, having fish frys and enjoying each other's company. Two particularly good friends were Jay and Audrey Gilbert from Hamilton, Montana. They were about ten years older than we were and Jay had taken up oil painting in Montana as a retirement hobby. He had never painted before but had a good teacher and was having considerable luck with his work, which he shared with me. He brought his paints with him and worked during the winter in Needles. I expressed some interest in this and Jay encouraged me to give it a try. I bought a bunch of paints and Jay walked me through my first painting as he passed along to me the many tips he had been learning from his excellent teacher at home.

I found it to be fun, challenging, time filling and a great retirement hobby. I discovered there was an art group in Needles that had been meeting for years, which had an excellent teacher who came twice a month from Las Vegas, Nevada, 100 miles away to teach this small class. He had been doing this for years. His name was Joe Mast and he has since passed away.

Joe charged a very small fee for his wonderful service, just about enough to pay for his gas for the trip. He was a professional artist who had degrees in art education. Aside from his knowledge and training, he was an excellent teacher who had a kind of way with students, but he rarely gave compliments on work. He would always objectively discuss how a work could be improved. This is far better and more helpful than empty compliments.

From that small beginning I have continued to paint in oils. I have now done 100 or more paintings and have sold or given away twenty or thirty. It has been a fun hobby and I think I have improved over the years. I am not ashamed to put a price on a piece of work and hope that someone will come along and want to buy it. I recommend painting as a wonderful retirement hobby.

Chapter 64

Alaska

Alaska is not only our largest state but one of the most interesting to visit. It has something for everyone—history, beauty, nature, and excitement. Bev and I have covered it in most every way possible and found it all to be thrilling.

We have taken a cruise ship from Los Angeles through the inside passage to Glacier Bay and back with stops all along the way. The inside passage is very narrow in many parts and from the perspective of an old navy man I was very much impressed with the navigation in such close quarters. By day it is great to see the sights along the way such as the whales in the water and the mountain goats on the steep hillsides of the fjords, all visible from the ship. The navigation beacons at night are lit up like Times Square. They are of every color, size and shape and are truly a maze to be mastered.

Glacier Bay is a magnificent fjord with glaciers coming down to the water from every side. The Muir, John Hopkins, and Margerie glaciers are the most active with continual calving of icebergs into the sea.

On another trip we had a truck and pulled a trailer all along the Alcan Highway. We drove all over British Columbia to get there. We went up the Caribou Highway (97) to Prince George where we turned west and took Highway 16 over to the coast to Prince Rupert where we caught the Alaskan Ferry, which is another great experience. If you have a passage ticket all the way to Haines you can get off the ferry at any and every stop along the way and stay overnight if you wish, then catch another ferry to continue your trip. The next day we stopped at Ketchikan and Juneau, and also at Wrangell and Petersburg which are small towns that the average traveler never sees.

As the ferry came into sight of Ketchikan, I noticed a lot of excitement on the beach south of town. I inquired as to the reason for all the commotion and discovered that folks were fishing for salmon which were running and the fishing was good. I bought a thirty-day fishing license and lure and within an hour of leaving the ferry I was fishing for salmon in Alaska. Within another hour I had caught my first Alaskan salmon in the ocean waters and altogether caught nine salmon in various areas of the state on that trip.

From Haines we drove over to Haines Junction and took the Alcan Highway into Alaska. We spent a month on that trip and drove practically every mile of paved road in Alaska and many, many miles of gravel and unpaved road.

We visited Fairbanks and played golf on the northernmost golf course in the world, or so we were told. We visited Denali National Park and saw Mount McKinley and many moose and grizzly bears. We visited the cities of Anchorage, Palmer, Seward, Homer, and Valdez.

After feeling that we had "seen it all," we headed back to the Yukon Territory in Canada on our way back to British Columbia.

The Alcan Highway was built during WWII as a war measure to provide a land passage between the lower 48 through Canada to Alaska. It was a dirt and

Vernon and Bev ready to meet the captain of the ship at his reception.

gravel road and really a tough drive. It has never been paved all the way through, but sections north and south of every village and town have been paved on either side a bit further from time to time. Canadians call it the Alaska Highway now.

There are many historical spots to be seen along the way. We visited Whitehorse, the entryway to the Yukon gold rush where Robert Service wrote some of his famous poems. The Alcan begins going north at Dawson Creek in British Columbia where there is a famous monument at "Mile O."

If one looks on a map, Dawson Creek is located in the far north of British Columbia so it is still a long, long way to travel south to Washington State. We came through many picturesque towns on our way home such as Kamloops and one named "Vernon" which had personal appeal to me.

We had several flat tires on the Alcan but carried spares. We also broke a spring but there always seemed to be a Good Samaritan who would stop and help. One such gentleman, who was a better mechanic than I, stopped and helped me get the spring apart and then took me to the next town to look for a replacement part. A 16-wheeler semi driver gave me a lift back to our rig where Bev was patiently awaiting my return. That was the only trouble we had on the mighty Alcan Highway.

I get brochures every week on tours and cruises to Alaska. One can take a cruise for as little as $650 per person and cruises are the deluxe way to go. Taking the Alaskan ferry system is a different and unique experience. They do have cabins aboard the ferry or one can sit up all night. I don't know whether you are adventurous enough to want to drive the Alcan, but you can fly to Anchorage or Fairbanks, rent a car and spent a couple of weeks seeing all of the major cities and sights of central Alaska. It is one of the greatest states and should not be missed.

Chapter 65

China

About twenty years ago we had an opportunity to go to China. We made the trip with Bev's brother and her sister-in-law, Fred and Lee Gillett. We are a very compatible foursome and have done the Mediterranean and other cruises together and it is always fun to travel with them. Comfortable travel companions are a must for a successful trip. We were part of a group of thirty so we fit on a bus nicely and were not too big a group to herd around.

Since China has opened their country to the western tourist trade they have developed certain facilities suitable to our tastes which limits what one can do according to the facilities available. I'm sure this has been expanded in the past ten years.

It is a long tedious flight across the Pacific any way you go and we flew from Los Angeles directly to Hong Kong. While in China we traveled by bus, train, and plane.

From Hong Kong we flew to Guilin in a rickety Russian-made plane seemingly held together with chewing gum. A few of the seats were broken and unusable which made for a very uncomfortable and scary flight. In the steward's widened aisle area there stood a refrigerator from what appeared to be a vintage 1935 Kelvinator. It was bolted to the floor and was the only receptacle for cold drinks and food.

In Guilin we took a cruise on the ancient and colorful Li River where we saw fisherman astride bamboo rafts using cormorant birds to catch their fish. Each bird has a ring around its neck and is attached to the fisherman by a cord. The cormorant dives for the fish but can't swallow the fish because of the ring around its neck. The fisherman pulls the bird in and takes the fish out of his beak—poor cormorant! The Yangtze River now also features river cruises that were not available when we were there twenty years ago.

We stayed in the Sheraton Guilin Hotel which was new and rated three stars, but the water from the faucets in our room was "non-potable." This blew my mind, however they did provide bottled water which we hoped was pure. From Guilin we flew to Xian where we saw the famous 2,200-year-old Terra Cotta army of 6,400 life sized soldiers that had been excavated only a short time before our visit.

Next we visited Shanghai where we strolled along the famous riverside Bund Promenade about which we had read in many novels centered in the Orient. From there we went to Beijing where we saw Tiananmen Square, also the Forbidden City and the Summer Palace. On another day we visited the Ming Tombs and walked on the Great Wall of China.

Shopping is an important part of every tour for Americans and others and considerable time is set aside for this activity. Bev and I are not shoppers. We go to see the sights, not to buy souvenirs. We go along with the tour and the group most of the time and try not to act like "ugly Americans," but we reach a saturation point rather quickly. We visited a cloisonné factory which was rather interesting seeing the young girls slaving in the sweatshop for pennies a day.

One afternoon we were making another "shopping" stop at a mall when I had reached my saturation point and called to our guide asking him to take us back to the hotel which he very kindly did. They went about ten minutes out of their way to take us to our hotel where they dropped us off then took the rest of the group back to the mall. Bev was running low on energy so opted for a quiet time in the room. I like to roam the streets by myself in any country to try and get the "feel" of the country, so I took off on a walk by myself. A few blocks away I ran into a large building that looked like a school to me, being a retired school administrator. I walked in the front door and since nobody challenged my being there I walked on through the halls peeking into classroom windows. It was primarily a music school and many rooms were full with from ten to twenty students of varying age groups sawing away on violins or tooting their horns. They appeared to be very accomplished students to me. I spent an enjoyable hour all by myself in this music school in the middle of Beijing where no one disturbed me.

One other experience impressed me greatly. China has over one billion in population which is far too many people for any country. Where there are too many people for the jobs and the food available there much be abject poverty. We read about it in all the great cities of the world such as Rio de Janeiro and Mexico City as well as Beijing. In my wandering I came across a building or solid wall a block long. All along this wall were hovels or shacks built out of scraps of cardboard, paper, or bamboo. Each one was approximately four or five feet out from the wall and maybe eight to ten feet long and about five feet high. In each of these sheds a family was living. They had no water, lights, or toilet facilities. They slept on the pavement of the street inside their shack. There was a husband and wife with three or four kids living their life in each tiny space. This was the most miserable poverty I have ever run into in my life. I don't know what they lived on or how they lived. They had no possessions, only scraps, trash and rags. And this wasn't just a few families, but hundreds of people in a city block or longer against the long wall.

I don't want to close on such a dreary note for we did have a wonderful trip and were able to visit a great country and culture we had never seen before. I do enjoy my solitary walks around a city outside the bounds of the travel group I am with. It is interesting that I was never accosted or questioned by any of the armed military personnel that were in evidence on every street.

Chapter 66

Galapagos Islands
Amazon Jungle
Machu Picchu

When one thinks of exotic places in the world one comes up with improbable names from far away places few of us ever expect to visit. Places such as Timbuktu, the Taj Mahal, Tierra del Fuego, or Tahiti.

Being an inveterate traveler I am always looking for somewhere new to visit. The farther away it is and the more esoteric, the better. We haven't spent much time in South America, but having good friends here in Oroville from Bolivia and Peru we felt we needed to explore that part of the world a little more

The Galapagos Islands are one of those faraway obscure places with an exotic name that an adventurer dreams about and hopes to visit some day. Everyone has seen the famous picture of Machu Picchu in the *National Geographic* or a travel magazine. It is another place for dreams

The Amazon River, second only to the Nile in length in the world, brings visions of jungle, headhunters, and canoes.

To imagine visiting any of these fantastic spots would be an explorer's heaven, but to combine all three into one trip seemed too much to hope for. But it can happen. Many travel companies combine all of the above three adventures into one package at a really reasonable price for what you get. These three spots are relatively close together after the long flight from the West Coast to Miami and then to Lima, Peru.

We made arrangements for this expedition about a year in advance traveling with my wife's brother and his wife, Fred and Lee Gillett. About a month before the trip was to take place I had some medical tests and the doctors said I was in need of open-heart surgery as soon as possible. I replied, "I have had the trip of a lifetime planned for a year now and it is set in cement." The cardiologist said "Well go ahead and see me as soon as you get back."

After visiting Lima, Peru, for a couple of days we flew across the Andes to our jungle camp. We were on the Tambopata River, a major tributary of the Amazon in the rain forest. We went up the river in a motorized canoe. Our camp was truly primitive as stated. There was no electricity or hot water. Our cabins were thatch-roofed and built high above ground to keep the varmints out—but the food was good. We took paddle canoe trips with about a three-inch freeboard to the water, as well as hikes through the rain forest with very competent and knowledgeable naturalist guides. At night we went out on the river in canoes with a very bright spotlight that picked out red alligator eyes from 200 yards away. The guide could then jockey the boat up to within twenty feet of the gator and we all could see him clearly in the spotlight. That was thrilling and something I had never experienced before.

From the jungle camp we flew to Cuzco, Peru, and Quito, Ecuador. Cuzco is 11,909 feet in elevation. Remember my heart condition!

From there we went to Machu Picchu and walked all over the ruins for the day. It was as exciting as it was purported to be and it was a stirring experience to walk where the Incas had lived hundreds of years ago. It is known as the "lost city of the Incas." Of course the natives always knew it was there but the first European to discover it was Hiram Bingham in 1911, so it had been kept a secret from the outside world since the Spanish invaders arrived.

We spent a couple of days on walking tours of Quito (only 9,000') and then went to the "Avenue of the Volcanoes" a valley flanked by volcanic cones in the Andes. Cotopaxi said to be the world's highest active volcano is 19,498 feet. They drove us as high as they could (about 15,000') and let us out to hike a couple of miles (downhill.) Remember my heart!!

From Quito we flew 600 miles west to the Galapagos Islands and meandered through them on a yacht. We snorkeled around reefs and swam with the sea lions. Remember my heart!!! We hiked all over the islands and saw colonies of the blue-footed boobies, land and marine iguanas, and at the Charles Darwin Research Station the famous Galapagos tortoises and the smaller saddle-backed tortoises.

I have used many superlatives in this exposition, but the Galapagos are truly beyond description. They exceed the travel brochure descriptions. You had to be careful in walking so you didn't step on the animals or nesting birds. The guides were very careful to keep you on the trails and you could walk only where they wanted you to, but as some of the birds nested right in the middle of the trail you had to step over them or around the eggs in the nests.

From the Galapagos we flew back to Gauyaquil, Ecuador, and from there back to the States. Can you imagine all of this adventure to such fantastic places for less than $5,000 per person? It can be done.

A week after our return to Oroville I had quadruple bypass heart surgery at Enloe Hospital. I guess the travel, altitude, hiking, and snorkeling put me in pretty good shape for the operation. I'm back to playing tennis for a couple of hours three days a week now and getting ready for our next adventure.

Chapter 67

Africa

If one is interested in geography, travel, and the world, the most exotic place in many people's minds is probably Africa. Every young man who has seen a Tarzan movie or read Hemingway's book on Kilimanjaro has probably dreamed of visiting Africa some day. It has certainly been on my "to do" list for a long time. Bev and I took a wonderful cruise from Barcelona, Spain, to Greece and Turkey covering the entire Mediterranean where we stopped at Cairo, Egypt, which is really on the African Continent but doesn't count for visiting deepest, darkest Africa.

A few years ago I read a wonderful brochure about a safari through Kenya and Tanzania and felt that my time had come for this sensational experience. As always, I invited Beverly to go with me, but she felt it was too difficult and primitive for her. When we were tent camping, the toilet was a hole in the ground with a three-legged stool sitting over it. The shower was a small tent with a bucket of hot water overhead which you could release by pulling a chain.

Looking for a partner I discussed the trip with my tennis buddy John Lonsdale, a retired lieutenant colonel from the US Air Force. His wife, Arlene, was not interested in going either so John and I joined forces as tent mates.

It is a long way from Oroville to the middle of

Africa. We made it to London nonstop and spent an interesting day there. Being tennis players, we took the tube out to visit the famous Wimbledon Stadium, as well as many other interesting sights before our plane took off that night.

Arriving in Nairobi, Kenya, we had a day of orientation at the famous Norfolk Hotel where Ernest Hemingway, Lord Baden Powell, and Teddy Roosevelt had stayed.

The next morning we took off in our English Land Rovers. There were four of us in each vehicle plus a driver. Our trip leader, Peter Giraudo, rode in a different truck each day so each group could benefit firsthand from his knowledge. The roof opened up so we could stand inside and shoot pictures of the animals.

We spent a day or two in different motel or hotel "camps" while the staff in a big truck went on ahead and set up a tent camp where we could spend a day or two. Then we would move on to another hotel camp while the staff broke down our tent camp and moved it on ahead to a new location.

In the camp we would be awakened by a staff member bearing a hot cup of tea and hot water to wash our faces. We each had a canvas container to wash in just outside our tent. Then we would go on an early morning game drive for a few hours. Upon returning to camp we would have breakfast in a covered and netted dining room. The rest of the day could be spent in various ways such as cleaning up, shaving, taking a shower, writing in a journal, writing cards and letters for home, and napping.

In the early afternoon we would go on another game drive until dark, having dinner on our return followed by the evening campfire.

Why do you go to Africa? To see the animals. We were certainly not disappointed. Our trip was everything that was promised and even more. We saw countless elephant, buffalo, zebra, rhinoceros, hippopotamus, baboon, cheetah, lion, hyena, giraffe, warthog, all kinds of antelope, and many birds including pelican, ibis, flamingo, stork, eagle, secretary bird, crane, hornbill, and starling. We also saw some weirdies like aardvark, mongoose, genet, jackal, and hyrax.

The guides were outstanding and seemed to know where every creature lived and took us right to them. We saw thousands of wildebeest or gnu migrating across the plains and elephants in the water as well as on land. We didn't keep count but on the last day our guide happened to mention that we had seen seventy-nine lions on our trip of three weeks.

We were within sight of Mount Kilimanjaro and Mount Kenya much of the time and visited noted historical and archeological sights where everything was very well explained as we went along.

We also enjoyed visiting very small villages and family compounds where we were able to mingle and trade with the local people and visit in their huts.

We were a small group of twelve people including women and two children who traveled in three Land Rovers all over Kenya and Tanzania for three weeks.

I hope this will encourage many of you who have had the "dream" to take advantage and make that wonderful trek to darkest Africa. It was the trip of a lifetime.

Chapter 68

The Taliban, Etc.

Everyone has something to say about terrorism and the Taliban since September and I thought I would like to throw in my two cents worth.

I have never knowingly met a terrorist or a member of the Taliban, and I have never been to Afghanistan or Pakistan, but I have been in some sixty other countries of the world, among them Muslim and Communist dominated countries.

Everyone who travels has a certain amount of trepidation when he leaves the homey comfort of the good old USA. One is immediately faced with different cultures, languages, customs, and regimes when traveling to any foreign country.

Although Bev and I have never gone out of our way to go into restricted or dangerous areas on the State Department lists, we have gone where we wanted to at the time. I thought I would recount a few of our experiences with some of the more autocratic civil servants we have run into in more totalitarian countries we have visited.

A few years ago we took a river cruise through the waterways of Russia from Moscow to St. Petersburg with some thirty other Oroville folks. We had a young Russian fellow on board with us who was our guard when we took day trips to see the sights. He was not a tourist guide in the usual sense but a guard to help us along our way to keep panhandlers or beggars from bothering us and to keep us from getting lost and to help us find our way back to the bus.

We were visiting Red Square in Moscow and enjoying taking pictures of St. Basil's Church and our group in the square in front of Lenin's tomb when three men dressed in black with dark trench coats accosted our guard and escorted him through a small door in the wall of the Kremlin. Many of us saw this happen and of course were concerned. He was friendly and we liked him and he was on our "side." Here we were isolated in the middle of the Kremlin in a Communist country and our "guide" had just been kidnapped and taken through a closed, unmarked door in the wall by Lenin's tomb. One doesn't know what to do in this kind of situation. Who can you turn to? Do you want to make a scene? Go and pound on the door? We took the path of least resistance and did nothing but mutter among ourselves, and lo and behold our friend turned up for dinner aboard ship that night. He didn't really know why they took him, but they checked his ID and all of his papers and checked with the cruise ship and were satisfied that he was who he said he was and that he belonged to our group so they released him.

These kinds of incidents makes one wonder about foreign travel especially since September 11, but I look on these events as the little things that add zest and excitement to a trip.

Another unusual incident occurred when Bev and I were driving our own car through the hinterlands of southern France. I have always been a fast driver "with the pedal to the metal" most of the time. We were on a two-lane highway that usually was the main street of every small town we traveled through. Dusk was falling and we were anxious to get to our destination. As we entered one small town at a rather fast clip a man in the street gave us the "slow down" sign. I casually waved to him and probably eased off a bit. That man may have been a good citizen who was warning me of the gendarme ahead or he may have been a policeman who had a phone to the other end of town. At any rate, we were about to get out of town when a genuine policeman in uniform with a sign stopped us. I know only a few words of French and "slow down" is not part of my vocabulary. He did not speak a word of English. We spent several minutes communicating by gestures, but I played real dumb and didn't know what he was trying to tell me. We both became increasingly frustrated. Finally he threw in a "langsam" which is a German word for slow. We had been living in Holland for a year and knew a few words of Dutch which is similar to German. A light flashed on, my face bore a big smile and I made him happy by nodding "yes … slow down." He was so glad that he had made his point that we both smiled and nodded at each other and he waved me along my way. No ticket!

Chapter 69

The Mighty Mississippi River

We recently took a cruise down the Mississippi from Memphis to New Orleans aboard the Delta Queen with a bunch of college friends. It was a very enjoyable experience and historical as well as interesting. The Delta Queen is the oldest and smallest of the fleet of paddle wheel steamboats run by the Delta Queen Steamboat Co. The cabins were tiny but all had a private bathroom.

The crew on board went overboard (pardon the expression) to be helpful, friendly, warm and personal with all of the passengers, with the exception of one person who must have been a drill sergeant somewhere along the line. They had an excellent five-piece band that played morning, noon, and night and added much to the festivities.

The food was excellent, some of the best we have ever had. I am generally a meat and potatoes man but everything was so good that I even ventured into frog legs and escargot for the first time in my life.

The Delta Queen was built in Stockton, California, in 1926 and is a National Historic Landmark. It was active in our Delta for many years and was a military ferry during WWII.

In 1946 Captain Tom Greene of the Greene Line got the "idea of broad jumping a million dollar 1,837-ton luxury paddle wheel steamer from the Pacific Coast to the cornfields of Illinois." She was towed

4,777 nautical miles through the Panama Canal to New Orleans where she was refurbished and entered into full service on the Mississippi for the Greene Line in 1948.

The river is one of the greatest geographical elements of the United States. It is hard to believe until you have experienced it. There is peace and quiet much of the time with only trees and bushes visible on either shore, as contrasted with much boat traffic with towboats (pushing) huge masses of barges all tied together, as well as oceangoing ships from Baton Rouge to New Orleans.

The trip is smooth compared to an ocean voyage even with a little wind and rain. It would be difficult to suffer seasickness on such an inland cruise.

Aside from shipboard activities which included everything from kite flying, trivia games, dancing and entertainment, to eating four times a day, there was much to see ashore of our great mid West, and well organized shore excursions were provided for tourists' enjoyment.

We flew from LAX to Memphis where we started our boat journey. We spent the night in the Peabody Hotel that is famous for the parade of ducks twice a day. The ducks have a pen on the roof of the hotel and each day at 11:00 A.M. they come down in an elevator and march to a beautiful fountain in the middle of the lobby where they spend the day. They march home at 5:00 P.M. daily and hundreds of people watch the parade each day. In fact, tour busses regularly make a stop at the Peabody just for this event which was started in the 1930s.

Memphis is also the home of Elvis and B.B. King. On a day tour we took before we sailed in the evening, we visited Graceland and museums with statues of Memphis's greatest kings, Elvis and B.B. We also saw the Lorraine Motel where Dr. Martin Luther King, Jr. was assassinated in 1968. His car still sits in front of the motel that is now the National Civil Rights Museum. We also walked up and down Beale Street "The Home of the Blues" which is like New Orleans Mardi Gras every night of the year.

The next day we were in Vicksburg, Mississippi. This was the site of one of the most crucial battles and sieges of the Civil War. Lincoln and the North knew they must control the Mississippi River to win the war and the tours emphasized the battles and siege.

We learned an interesting fact there: casinos are popular and plentiful all along the river. There were various laws and regulations; some must be floating and are built like our riverboat, but they don't have an engine and just sit in their little pond on the river. Harrah's has a seven-story casino in Vicksburg and is one of four major casinos located there. Vicksburg, incidentally, is now on the Yazoo River a tributary of the Mississippi as the river has changed course continually over the years.

Natchez is noted for its 200 antebellum homes. The tours will take you through several as well as to a plantation and cotton gin. Each of the homes has a name. We visited "Rosalie" located on a high bluff overlooking the river on a site chosen by the French for their first settlement on the river in 1716 and named Fort Rosalie.

One of our enthusiastic fellow travelers fell down while dancing and broke his collarbone so the boat called 911. It is interesting that these boats can put up against the bank almost anywhere along the river. We made an unscheduled stop in Greenville at a nice park along the river much like Bedrock Park here in

Oroville. An ambulance met the boat and they took the passenger off in a gurney and then to the hospital along with the purser. After treatment they rented a car and rejoined the boat downriver the next day. This provided a little unexpected excitement for the day while underway.

On our trip down the Mississippi River we were in Tennessee and Mississippi going through the heartland of America. Baton Rouge, Louisiana, is Huey Long country. Every tour guide or person you meet has a story to tell about Huey. The big corporations hated him but the common people revered him and they still do today. He was at the height of his power in the 1930s. Louisiana is oil country and the refineries and big companies were not paying any states taxes. Huey changed that and used the money to improve the roads, schools, and to benefit the average citizen. He built the state capitol building as a copy of the Empire State Building. Huey is buried on the grounds beneath a big statue of himself. He built the governor's mansion as a copy of the White House as he was heading in that direction and wanted to get used to living there. However, former Governor Huey P. Long was assassinated in the lobby of the state capitol in 1935.

Our boat was docked about 100 yards from the restored WWII destroyer USS *Kidd* named for Rear Admiral Kidd who was killed aboard his flagship the USS *Arizona* during the Japanese attack on Pearl Harbor. It and an extensive military museum were just a step from our boat and provided a memorable experience for all WWII sailors.

We were ashore in St. Francisville, Louisiana, on the one day of the year they honor a touching event from the Civil War with a parade through town and a big celebration. They call it "the day the war stopped."

In 1863 the USS *Albatross* was shelling low-lying Bayou Sara and St. Francisville atop the bluffs. Lt. Commander John E. Hart, captain of the *Albatross* was killed. Hart was a Mason as were other officers aboard. They wanted to bury their commander ashore rather than in the river waters. A boat was sent ashore under a flag of truce to inquire if there were any Masons in town. It so happened one of the oldest lodges in the state was in St. Francisville. A Confederate Brother arranged for the Masonic funeral. The crew struggled up from the waterfront with Hart's body and he was buried in the Grace Episcopal Churchyard with all due respect being paid by Union and Confederate soldiers alike.

The day we visited there we noticed Masons in aprons and uniforms from all over Louisiana and other states as well, and they were going to reenact the burial service as it had occurred in 1863.

In New Orleans our hotel was located in the French Quarter so we were able to walk all around in that area and enjoy its sights. Since the water table is so high, all of the cemeteries are above ground and quite different and colorful from what we are used to.

Something else new to us were the so called "shotgun houses." These were inexpensive houses that were being built about 1900. They had one door in the middle of the house front and one window, or if it was a duplex it had just two doors and two windows centered on the front. There was a hall straight through the house from the front door to the back door with rooms on either side off of that hallway. It was said that if you fired a shotgun through the front door it would go straight through the house and out the back door without hitting anything. Many of these houses are well preserved and maintained and still lived in. Some of the same style may still be built today.

In the afternoon as we were preparing to head for the airport and home it began to rain hard and the streets were awash as we left the hotel. This was the beginning day of the flood that devastated Texas and Louisiana. We were lucky to get away from that area on the first day of the big rain.

Chapter 70

Serendipity

The trip down the Mississippi River was taken with fifteen friends from college. This was a bonus that made the entire trip extra fun as we had our own group on board. A long time ago fourteen girls living in the same dormitory at Occidental College started a "round-robin" letter upon graduation and this letter has been going continuously for over fifty years. Every couple of years or so this group, along with their husbands, organize a little reunion trip for those who are able to go. That was the occasion for this river cruise. Twelve of the women are still alive. Five have been widowed. Two have been divorced, and the other seven are with their original husbands including my wife and me.

Serendipity is one of my favorite words. The dictionary defines it as "the gift of finding valuable or agreeable things not sought for." I think of it in scientific terms as in a researcher looking for a cure for cancer perhaps, but in his experiments he discovers penicillin. That, then, is a serendipitous discovery that was not expected. It happened by a lucky chance.

In my travels around the world some of my fondest experiences have occurred by lucky chance or serendipity. In other words, these incidents were not scheduled in the itinerary of the trip.

One such incidence occurred in the Peabody Hotel in Memphis, Tennessee. We met a couple while we were having a bite to eat. To start a conversation you might ask where people are from. They answer, "California." "Where in California?" They answer "LA." As I am a retired educator I am always interested in where people went to school, so I usually ask. I attended Hollywood High School. The gentleman informed us he was from Fairfax High which is the next school west of Hollywood. His wife mentioned she attended Marshall. This happens to be the next school on the east end of Hollywood and coincidentally was the first school at which I taught and where I was head football coach. Now, how is that for a chance meeting of three people all from adjacent Hollywood schools and coincidentally the first school at which I taught and where I was head football coach. It is like graduates of Oroville, Las Plumas, and Prospect High schools running into each other in a far corner of the world even though they didn't know one another here in Oroville.

I recounted the story of "the day the Civil War stopped" to bury a Union sailor in the Confederacy. Now, wasn't it pure serendipity that we visited St. Francisville, Louisiana, on the one day of the year when they were celebrating this event with a parade and reenactment of the burial of Commander Hart so that we could participate in and enjoy this special day of the year in town?

Once, in an elevator in Paris, France, I heard people speaking English and upon further conversation discovered they, too, were graduates of Hollywood High School. Serendipity?

All of the crew of the Delta Queen wore polished gold nametags. We were sitting in the lounge one day having a cup of coffee while most of the passengers were ashore. There was a gentleman sitting near us with a badge on and I could make out that his name was Jim. I said "What do you do aboard, Jim?" He replied "I'm the chief pilot." We spent the next hour in a most informative discussion of the river, steamboats, pilots, etc. We learned more about the river than anyone else aboard. In Mark Twain's time the pilots were more important and made more money than the captain. Pilots know every twist and turn of the river, every sandbar, wreck, and marker buoy. The captain was more concerned with the passengers and cargo and whether the boat was making money. Today the captain has the ultimate responsibility for the entire ship and its safety and makes more money than the pilot, but there is a pilot on duty twenty-four hours a day. We were moored at a dock, but Jim was on duty while he was drinking coffee with us in the lounge. The pilothouse is where the pilot works. It is not called a bridge as in the navy but there are flying bridges on each side so the pilot or master can look over the sides. Pilots take examinations for each twenty-mile segment of the river. They are given a blank piece of paper and must draw their segment of the river with every curve, marker, and buoy in its correct place.

There are paddle wheel cruises on the Ohio River from Pittsburg to Cincinnati to Memphis and over to Nashville and Chattanooga as well as on the upper Mississippi to Minneapolis and St. Paul and over to Chicago. Jim is a qualified pilot on every inch of all these rivers. It was a real pleasure spending a quiet informative hour with him. Serendipity? Yes!

We have also cruised the Columbia and Snake rivers in our Pacific Northwest with this same Occidental College group. I would certainly recommend a trip with the Delta Queen Steamboat Company. It is fun and there is much to see and do. Contact your local travel agent.

Chapter 71

The Bear and I

I've been retired now for thirty-three years and I like to say that I haven't done a lick of work in all that time or earned a nickel to add to my social security. This isn't entirely true but makes a pretty good story.

For the first few years of retirement we spent our time traveling around the United States, western Canada, and Alaska. One year we spent most of our summer touring our great national parks and monuments of the Southwest. This included the Grand Canyon, Canyon de Chelly, Zion, Canyonlands, Arches, Grand Teton, Yellowstone, etc.

We took many nature walks with park rangers and always attended the evening campfire programs. As I observed these "mostly" young men and women naturalists leading these walks and programs, I said to myself, "I can do that." So I inquired about how to apply for one of those positions and obtained application forms before the summer was over. When I returned home that fall I did apply and was selected the following summer as a campground ranger at Sequoia National Park here in California. Most seasonal rangers are college students who are available during the summer and many young schoolteachers who are out of school for the summer. There are a few old timers around who have been spending their summers as rangers for many years, but about 85 percent are

National Park Ranger Vernon orients a back country hiker in Sequoia National Park, 1983.

young people under the age of thirty. Of course, the government cannot discriminate in hiring because of age, so when I was hired I considered myself as their token senior citizen. I was about fifty-nine or sixty when I was selected. I spent the first summer as a campground ranger and then worked my way up to a "naturalist-interpreter" which was a more prestigious job and the one that I really wanted. I spent a total of five seasons with the National Park Service just before moving to Oroville.

We received excellent on-the-job training from the park service. Although I had a biology minor in college and many qualifications for the job, the orientation and training program for new rangers was thorough in providing information about the local park, rules and regulations, local flora and fauna, etc. Each naturalist had to develop his own slide show on a subject of his choice for his campfire program.

At that time Sequoia had one of the highest records of any national park in the United States in the number of bear contacts, incidents of automobile break-ins and other bear confrontations.

I had spent forty years backpacking in the High Sierra and had had many bear contacts throughout those years. During my five years in Sequoia I was involved in shooting one bear, tranquilizing several and helping to measure, weigh, and put radio collars on the bears. I enjoyed working with the animals and volunteered for these kinds of experiences whenever I had a chance.

Sequoia was one of the first parks to install bear-proof food storage metal boxes at every campsite in the park. The rule for campers was to keep all their food in these boxes and keep them locked at all times. No food was to be stored in automobiles including trunks, and no food or dirty dishes were to be left out on tables.

Special law enforcement rangers, with police powers, carried guns, but all of the regular rangers carried radios most of the time and were on call for emergencies, and could also report problems to the park dispatching system whenever they came across them.

Vernon works with a tranquilized bear in Sequoia National Park.

One day during my last year in the park this sixty-four-year-old, white-haired ranger received a call on his radio that there was a bear in the campground at site 156 in the middle of the day. I was afoot and had no transportation, but I was in that vicinity and reported to the site as soon as I could get there.

A family had just arrived and was setting up their campsite. They were putting up their tent, unloading their car, getting out their camping equipment, assembling their stove, etc. They were in the process of moving their food from their car to their bear box when this very cagey bear arrived on the scene. Bears are very smart animals. They know where people keep their food. They have learned how to smash out windshields, climb into cars, tear out the back seat to get into the trunk, open ice chests, and get a free lunch whenever they can. They also teach all of these learned tricks to their cubs so they pass these bad habits on from one generation to another. This is a major problem in all of our national parks where humans and bears cohabit. The bears are far smarter than a city family with little children who may be visiting a bear-infested national park for the very first time. The new campers don't understand the seriousness of the problem despite the signs, brochures, and pamphlets they receive giving proper camping and bear-proofing instructions.

The family involved in this incident had moved most of their food to the bear box. The food was in the box, on the box, or in front of the box when the bear arrived on the scene. The folks had not had a chance to lock their box yet. Ranger Carter arrived on the scene as the bear was having a grand lunch in front of the box. Approved methods of chasing a bear are to holler at him, throwing rocks or pine cones at him, clap your hands, wave your arms, and tell him to go away. I did all of these things and the bear moved off twenty-five to fifty yards as I started to throw all of the food into the bear box.

There is a comfort level between all animals and other predators like humans. A flock of geese will sit in a field or on a pond until a hunter approaches to a certain distance and then they will take flight. Little birds around the yard are the same way and all animals and humans are the same. After moving off about fifty yards, the bear decided to come back and get another bite of lunch. Now my comfort level with an approaching bear is about twenty-five yards, so as he approached, I backed off to my twenty-five-yard range. The bear started eating again and I started my noise-making maneuvers including throwing rocks and moving back towards the bear. As I got within his comfort zone, fifteen to twenty yards, he turned and ran away again. I grabbed some more food and stuffed it in the bear box. While this game was being played out about fifty campers had gathered in a wide circle watching the sport. No one offered to help make noise or throw rocks, but they were enjoying the show. This tug-of-war match went on about four or five times. I wasn't about to give up or quit although I backed up every time the bear came back and approached me at the box. The bear finally did give up and took off across the campground and back toward the woods. I was successful in getting the rest of the food into the bear box and getting it locked up with the big chain provided. I don't recall even getting a round of applause from the assembled group of onlookers, but I was satisfied as I had successfully done the job I was hired to do. At the end of that summer, however, I quit the National Park Service and moved to Oroville where I have continued my retirement in a more sedate way. I'm still not working for a living.

A bear prowls the campground.

Bear-damage to a car.

A bear box where food should be kept.

Up a tree where the bear belongs.

We release a bear back to the wild.

A biologist works with a bear.

Chapter 72

Traveling with Irv

I rv never learned to read. He was an invalid as a child with an infected knee. He was confined to a wheelchair until he was ten or eleven years old. When he was about ten, he went to school in his wheel chair where he was placed in the first grade. He was ridiculed by the teacher and students and soon dropped out. Irv attended a few years in high school, where he was successful in some shop classes but still could not read.

Irv was a success in life. He married, raised four children, held numerous jobs, such as mechanic and security guard, and was able to adapt to his lack of literacy as many other people do.

Irv enrolled in adult reading programs several times in New Jersey but was never successful. Either the material used was not right for him, or he didn't hit it off with his instructor.

Irv's wife died a few years ago, and he moved to Oroville to live with his brother on Pomona Street. He made another attempt to learn to read by going to the Oroville Library on Mitchell Street and enrolling in their Laubach literacy program.

I saw an article in the paper a few years ago calling for volunteers for the reading program and participated in their training seminar presented by Jeanette Richard, the library literacy specialist, and her assistant Sandra Woodson of the Oroville Library. It was some time before they called me, but when Irv signed up they thought we would be a good match.

We spend more than a year reading together twice a week in one and two hour sessions. Irv has come a long way, but he still has a long way to go to become an independent reader.

Irv can now read material such as this !

Irv decided that living with his brother was not working out and that he wanted to move back to his home turf in New Jersey. He is not comfortable following road maps and felt that driving across country was beyond his capability at age sixty-four. There was no one in his family who was available to drive across country with him.

Irv and I had developed a good rapport with each other over the last year and had become good friends. Irv asked me if I would consider driving across the country with him. He would pay expenses and give me an airplane ticket to return home.

This kind of commitment was not included on the agenda of the reading program when I took the seminar. I'm sure this is beyond the usual relationship between students and volunteer reading instructors. I gave the invitation much soul searching and finally agreed to accompany Irv. It wouldn't cost me anything but a week of my time, and I felt I would be helping someone who had a real need. I knew I was making a commitment of considerable responsibility, but I was willing to do this.

Irv's plan was to drive straight through day and night in three days without stopping—we'd be sleeping in the car while the other fellow was driving.

My wife and I had tickets to the community band concert at the State Theater on the Fourth of July. I didn't want to miss this event, so we planned to leave after the program.

We left Oroville at 5:00 P.M. on July 4. Our first stop was in Truckee where we visited my son Bob and my two grandchildren for a few minutes. I didn't realize that the western states of Nevada, Utah, Wyoming, and Nebraska now have seventy-five mile per hour speed limits. We could put the cruise control on seventy-five and be legal and still cover lots of ground in Irv's secondhand Mercury, which he had bought in Oroville. The car performed perfectly and we didn't have a bit of car trouble on the entire trip.

We arrived in Salt Lake City at 4:00 A.M. We had covered 1,272 miles in twenty-four hours. We asked some folks where to eat, and they recommended a good local family restaurant. Imagine our surprise when we opened our menu to the dinner page to find a business card advertisement as follows: "Irv and Vern Construction Inc." What a coincidence and what a small world we live in. Serendipity?

We were lucky with weather all the way across the country. We did have a little rain as we left Nebraska and went into Iowa. From Iowa east the speed limit was sixty-five in all states. It was then the middle of the night and visibility was poor in the rain so we stopped at a rest stop and we both got a couple of hours of solid sleep in the car which helped alleviate our fatigue.

I had two general impressions of our drive across the United States. One was the wonder of our magnificent interstate highway system. We went nearly all the way on I-80 and I was continuously amazed observing the shining ribbon of concrete extending way ahead of us with perhaps twenty miles in view in the wide-open Western states. My other observation was that it seemed like the entire highway from coast to coast was under construction for repairs during these summer months. Many, many repair jobs were under way and the road narrowed to one lane each way for miles and miles with a forty miles per hour or less speed limit.

We hit 2,000 miles just below Chicago at 11:00 A.M. of the second day. I was not aware of the turnpike system in Indiana and Ohio. They go clear across each state and connect directly with each state on I-80. Of course each state wants to collect its toll so there were booths at the exit of each state. The roads are two lanes in each direction and when you near the tollbooths, traffic backs up from three to five miles and it took from a half hour to forty-five minutes to get through each booth. This drove me crazy and I don't think California would stand for this kind of delay for a minute. All it would take to correct it would be to widen the road to four lanes for two or three miles and install more booths and collectors. I think of the California Agriculture Inspection station at Truckee. I go through there quite often and there is never a wait of more than four or five cars.

By the third night we were both suffering from sleep deprivation and decided to check into a motel after we had gotten on the Pennsylvania Turnpike. We stopped near Pittsburgh about midnight and slept soundly until 6:00 A.M. That helped a lot.

Irv has emphysema, a heart condition, and is a diabetic. He checks his blood sugar twice a day and is very careful about taking his insulin pills and eating on schedule. He also has bad legs from his childhood infection. This did present some problems in timing our stops in towns for meals, etc.

We hit the road at 8:00 A.M. on the last day, July 7, and it was a fairly easy day after the six hours of sleep. We arrived in Vineland, New Jersey, at 3:00 P.M.—seventy hours after leaving Oroville. Irv was glad to be back in his home state of New Jersey where he has brothers, sisters, and children. He knows his way around the southern part of New Jersey very well and is comfortable driving near home. I hope he enrolls in another reading program and builds on the good foundation he has developed in California.

I knew that traveling with Irv would be an experience and an adventure and it was in every respect. It will probably be the last time I ever drive across our great country, but two old goats successfully made it all the way in seventy hours without an accident or car breakdown.

Chapter 73

Celebrating Fifty Years

We were married in Pasadena, California, in 1947. On our fiftieth wedding anniversary in 1997, we decided to celebrate by taking all of our children and grandchildren on the little "Love Boat" for a weekend cruise from Los Angeles to Mexico via Catalina Island. Included were Bob and Nikki Carter and their children Demi and Taylor of Truckee, and Deanna and Joe Russomano and their children Shanti, Kendra and Faith of Fresno.

Bev's brother Fred and wife Lee have enjoyed many travels with Bev and Vernon.

On the cruise the first stop was Catalina Island. This had a special meaning as I was a policeman in Avalon during one summer's vacation from teaching school in 1951. Deanna and Bob were one and two years old at the time.

The next stop was Ensenada, Mexico. Our family had spent a lot of time at Estero Beach water skiing and camping when the children were teenagers. Estero is about nine miles south of Ensenada, and we hired a bus to take us down there to renew old memories.

This brief trip was a wonderful way to celebrate our Golden Wedding Anniversary with the entire family. They all enjoyed reminiscing about events in their lives while they were growing up, and sharing these memories with the next generation of children.

As this book is being compiled in 2009, we Carters have been married sixty-two years. Our baby boy Bobby turned 60 this year. We're both healthy with few medical problems. Any problems that come up are being controlled by doctors and medication. I still play tennis three days a week and Beverly plays golf once a week. We maintain our own home by doing our own housekeeping and gardening. We gather, split, and saw up three or four cords of firewood every year, together, which keeps us warm during the winters with a wood stove.

We are active in community affairs. We attend the Community Concert series every year. We are both active members of the Optimist Club, I volunteer at church and at the public library for other civic events. This year I also volunteered to count the homeless, as I have done in the past.

I worked for the 1990 US Census and have signed up to participate again in 2010. I will probably work for the 2020 census as well.

We have been goal-oriented all of our lives together. We are now eighty-five years of age and my goal is to live to be 100. I feel that is a cinch since it is only fifteen more years down the road!

Chapter 74

Traveling with Faith

I took my nine-year-old granddaughter Faith on an Elderhostel trip. Elderhostel? You may ask. "I thought that was for senior citizens?" This was a very special trip. It was called intergenerational—which is a big word that simply means two generations, grandparents with grandchildren. The children's ages are limited from nine to twelve. We attended at Squaw Valley Academy, California, and the program was titled "Tahoe Sierra Natural History with your Grandchild." There were thirteen youngsters and twenty adults in the one-week program, and we all had a good time. It is great meeting people from all over the country. In our program there were people from Florida to Seattle to Maryland, and it was fun observing the interrelations between the families and the thirteen young people.

Lolita was there. She was a ten-year-old vamp with all the moves of a twenty-three-year-old vixen. She had been at the pool all summer and had a golden tan. She was cute and knew it and made a move on the most mature twelve-year-old boys. They enjoyed the constant attention for a while, but by the end of the week I think she was becoming a bit wearing. The book among the adults was that she would lose her virginity at about age twelve, and would be an unwed mother at about age fifteen. One wonders whether her grandparents could see this kind of behavior as easily as we objective outsiders could.

Gary Cooper was there. He was the embodiment of Lou Gehrig and Jack Armstrong, the all-American boy. Let's call him Mike. He was a good-looking twelve year old with a great personality. He was calm, pleasant, happy and nice to all the other kids, grandparents, and even Lolita. He was a pleasure to have around, just a good kid who was his own man and enjoyed life. He participated in everything and pulled his own weight each day.

Then there was Amy, the youngest sister in *Little Women* and the personification of shyness. She never smiled once all week. Of course she had a full set of braces on her teeth, but that is no excuse. She was a physically mature twelve year old just touching puberty, but that is no excuse either. She didn't participate much in the activities that were planned just for the children and sometimes would be the only child sitting in a lecture with the adults while the other kids were participating in an outside activity. She was a totally introverted child and didn't relate to either adults or children. We all felt very sorry for her and wondered how her life will turn out and if she will ever learn to talk to people. She can't spend her life sitting between two grandparents.

My granddaughter Faith was one of the youngest, smallest, and least sophisticated children at the camp. We did a lot of hiking and chose among three groups—fast, moderate, and slow hikers. Being a little unsure of herself, Faith chose the slow group the first day but by noon she had graduated to the middle group. For the rest of the week she and Grandpa were in the fast group, and she was at the front of the pack. Faith did KP duty, made her own sandwiches and lunch, picked up her dishes after meals and participated in all the group activities. This grandpa was mighty proud of her.

Elderhostel is an educational adventure for adults fifty-five and older. It was started in 1957 in New England and is now countrywide and international. Besides the regular programs, which are educational, they have service programs where individuals volunteer to help other organizations and projects. The intergenerational program for kids and grandparents is fairly new but now nationwide.

I have attended several Elderhostel programs with my wife, several service programs, and an international service program in Indonesia. Based on our experience in Squaw Valley, I would certainly recommend any of the Elderhostel programs to anyone over fifty-five who is looking for an educational adventure.

Chapter 75

Paris on $600?

Can you believe a week in Paris with round trip air fare, six nights hotel room, six breakfasts in your hotel, a boat ride on the Seine River, a diamond gem show, a free fashion show and time for sightseeing all for around $600? If you don't believe such an exceptional deal, check with Lanny Dragon at Mission Travel on Fifth Avenue, Oroville. He has sent over 130 people from Oroville and environs to Paris for a week during the past couple of months, and another group is on their way this week.

I heard about it from the radio on station KEWE. I was talking to my granddaughter in Fresno on the telephone one night and she remarked, "I would just love to go to Europe." I said, "Why don't you go to Paris for a week? It only costs $600 from Oroville." She said, "That sounds great, I can afford that."

She rounded up three of her friends and her sister, all in their twenties who likewise wanted to go and she called me back and said, "Grandpa, why don't you go with us and be our tour guide?" My bags are always packed and I wasn't busy that week so I decided to go with them. I've been to Paris several times and it is my favorite city in the world so I was looking forward to the trip.

Another friend of mine heard about the trip and formed a group of twenty-three people to go with her. One couple, who had formerly lived in nearby Magalia, but have since moved to the Lake of the Ozarks in Missouri, heard about it and they flew from there to Oakland to join her group.

Traveling with the group of twenty-year-old young people was a little different from traveling with senior citizens, so I had a few experiences I didn't expect. The youngsters were enthralled with the Eiffel Tower, probably because it was the most familiar landmark they knew. It was the first place we visited and they wanted to go back every day and see it by sunrise, sunset, and after dark. I had been on the Eiffel Tower before but never felt the necessity to go clear to the top, but sure enough they dragged me to the tiptop this time. The fee is about $2 to the first level, $4 to the second level, and $10 for an elevator ride all the way to the top. Although it was a rather smoggy day, we saw all of Paris as it is laid out before us like a relief map. Major attractions are easily identified such as the Arc de Triomphe, Sacre-Cour Church, Notre Dame Cathedral, and Hotel des Invalides which is Napoleon's tomb. It is a magnificent sight and we didn't have to wait in line to get to the top.

We spent a lot of time on the Metro, their subway system, and it is easy to get around once you learn the system. A single ride is $1.88 and you can stay underground all day for that price if you don't go outside an exit gate. Ten passes bought at a time are only $8.66 so that cut our price in half. As there were six of us we got every third ride free by using this system.

I did many other things I wouldn't have done as a result of being with the young people. I ate dinner at the Hard Rock Café and had a hamburger at the McDonalds on the corner by our hotel. I attended a ladies fashion show at the Printemps department store which is similar to I. Magnin's or Sak's Fifth Avenue. I shopped and shopped for Paris fashions at shops, stores, and boutiques, the girls bought several dresses for themselves and friends. I haven't been in a music store for years, but I spent quite a bit of time in the Virgin Record store. It was a new experience for me. The kids bought several CDs in Paris. One granddaughter had brought several CDs, a player, and earphones from home so she wouldn't be lonely.

We did many of the traditional tourist attractions. We spent a half-day in the Louvre and then visited the D'Orsay Museum where they had moved all the impressionist paintings into that old railroad station. The entrance fee to the museums is about $8 these days. The girls' hotel was up near the Sacre-Cour Church and we hiked all the way down the Champs Elysses from the Arc de Triomphe to the Place de la Concorde which is quite a walk.

Our boat ride on the Seine was very relaxing and enjoyable. The river was very high from mountain and rain runoff, the larger boats were running, and it was a free ride included in our package. The boat was full and those left over had to wait for the next one an hour later.

We had lunch one day near the Louvre at a very popular restaurant. The toilet was downstairs in the basement. It was alright, but old fashioned. I took a couple of the girls with me to the restroom. There was just one toilet stall and an exposed urinal against one wall. I was using the urinal as a lady came out of the cubicle. The washbasin was directly behind me and as she washed her hands, she and I were standing back to back with no apparent embarrassment or false modesty on her part. The girls looked in the closet, but with just a hole in the floor, they didn't want any part of that.

All in all it was a wonderful trip and exactly as advertised. We were fortunate in having excellent weather all week, with showers only one afternoon. The price is so reasonable you can't afford to stay home. You can't spend a week in San Francisco for that price.

Chapter 76

Epilogue

This journey has taken eighty-five years so far. The writing about it has occurred over the past twenty years and has needed much revision to bring it up to date. It has been a good life, exciting for me, and I think a bit unusual from the norm.

I certainly made the right choice when Beverly and I got married. It has been sixty-three years. She has been my lover, friend, partner, helpmate, and typist. We have shared all of the experiences in this book together and I could not have accomplished half of what I have done without her help and care. I don't know where the accolades are due in a book, but I give them to her from my heart.

Our son Bob has grown into a fine man who has operated his own rock blasting business for many years in Truckee. He is a mountain climber who has scaled El Capitan in Yosemite Valley a dozen times. He is an expert hang glider, and a world class downhill ski racer. (109 miles per hour timed on skis.) He participated in a Mount Everest climbing and hang gliding expedition. Last year he was president of the Truckee Optimist Club and you know how close this is to my heart. Bob should write a book too!

Our daughter Deanna is the sharpest one of the family. She has had many jobs in many lines of work, and within the first few weeks of a new job, she is the number one employee and running the company. She has given us three lovely granddaughters. None of our family has married at an early age—we have all been married in the mid or late twenties. Nevertheless, two of Deanna's daughters, Shanti and Kendra, gave us two great grandchildren last year so there are four generations living now.

If you have read this book through you may have gathered that I have been goal-oriented all of my life. As I've said, now that I have reached age eighty-five my latest goal is to live to be 100 years old. That is only fifteen years away and achievable.

Bev and I are both in good health for this stage in our lives. She plays golf every week and I play tennis three days a week and do a lot of heavy yard work on the other days.

I hope our family and close friends have enjoyed reading about our journey.

LaVergne, TN USA
24 November 2009
165152LV00005B/2/P